THE
BASEBALL STADIUM
GUIDE

Written by Iain McArthur
Designed by Daniel Brawn

The first ballgame I watched in-person was a 1989 NLCS contest between the San Francisco Giants and the Chicago Cubs at Candlestick Park, and I've been hooked on baseball and its ballparks ever since. As well as being a ballpark chaser, I have watched at least 17 other sports in over a dozen countries, spanning five continents.

I regularly contribute to Football Weekends magazine in the UK and am currently developing a book about my multiple world-wide sporting loves.

In addition to sports, I also write extensively about my other passion - rock and metal music - for Rockfiend.

I would like to thank Dan Brawn for his outstanding and stylish design work and Angus Reid of Pillar Box Red Publishing Ltd for making this book happen.

This book is dedicated to my wife, my son and his partner, and my gorgeous wee granddaughter. Additional thanks also go to all of the friends and family members who have accompanied me on my musical and sporting adventures over the years.
Iain McArthur

© 2023. Published by Aspen Books, an imprint of Pillar Box Red Publishing Ltd. Printed in India.

ISBN: 978-1-914536-71-7

THE BASEBALL STADIUM GUIDE

We call them stadiums but there's definitely something special about the friendly confines of a ballpark. They're not like the caustic rectangles where they play football or the antagonistic indoor boxes where they play hockey. No, a ballpark is somewhere to sit in the sun for a few hours - maybe with a small stretch about seven innings in - while the beauty and drama of America's national pastime gently unfolds before you.

Each park has its own style and ambience. They can be quirky and asymmetrical, maybe with green monstrous fences and ivy, or city skylines and riverbanks, but there's always lush, green grass or whatever impersonates grass in the sun-less domes that remain.

They're not just buildings. Living, breathing crowds inhabit the ballpark for pageantry and passion; to eat peanuts and crackerjacks, and root-root-root for the home team. They are the warm, safe place where the boys of summer take turns to joust with triumph and disaster and accept the outcome with a tip of the cap or a slow trudge back to the dugout.

There's noise from anthem singers and organists and beer vendors' sales-pitches, but it all stops for the crack of the bat and the arc of the ball in the bright blue yonder; squinting to see if it will be plucked from the sky or soar over the fence, or maybe even carry on out of the park altogether with a splash.

This is the story of the 13 Parks, ten Fields, five Stadiums, one Centre and one Coliseum where they play baseball in 2023. There are still two old jewel boxes left but they've had a few facelifts. The era of multi-sport enormo-domes in out-of-town parking lots is over and we've gone back to the future with downtown retro-parks and modern techno-parks with retractable roofs and 'villages' attached.

Some of these ballparks are new and have yet to write their story, but some will soon be destroyed, once the suits and moneymen decide their fate. The movie now is not so much "If you build it, they will come" but rather; "if you don't build it, they will go".

This book is about architecture, pennants and heroes who end up on statues. It is also about traditions, mascots, songs, curses, rally squirrels, famous fans, sausage races, ceremonial first-pitches and fried bull's testicles.

Play ball.

CONTENTS

6	Chase Field
8	Truist Park
10	Oriole Park at Camden Yards
14	Fenway Park
18	Wrigley Field
22	Guaranteed Rate Field
26	Great American Ball Park
30	Progressive Field
34	Coors Field
38	Comerica Park
42	Minute Maid Park
46	Kauffman Stadium
48	Angel Stadium
50	Dodger Stadium
54	loanDepot Park
56	American Family Field
60	Target Field
64	Citi Field
68	Yankee Stadium
72	Oakland Coliseum
74	Citizens Bank Park
78	PNC Park
82	Oracle Park
86	Petco Park
90	T-Mobile Park
94	Busch Stadium
98	Tropicana Field
100	Globe Life Field
102	Rogers Centre
106	Nationals Park

'The BOB'

Chase Field

Pheonix, AZ

With Spring Training and the Arizona Fall League already established, the Diamondbacks' arrival in 1998 brought almost year-round baseball to Metro Phoenix. Unfortunately, summer here is too hot for an open-air park, so roofed stadiums in hot-spots like Tampa Bay, Miami and Texas are more practical designs than classic retro ballparks. Nonetheless, the neat red brick and green steel exterior, and an artistic rotunda help to disguise the Astrodome-sized warehouse effect. Wall panels can swivel to allow the desert breeze in and a solar pavilion provides power and shade.

Whilst air-con is essential, the park doesn't absolutely need a swimming pool, but why not? The Pool Suite is situated just behind the fence in right-center, so home run balls are an occasional hazard; as are pool-hoppers. The D-Backs jumped in after clinching the NL West in 2011 and the Dodgers made an unwelcome appearance two years later.

The Diamondbacks have been slow to draw fans back after Covid, with pre-pandemic attendances in 2019 considerably higher than post-pandemic. Visiting fans sometimes outnumber home fans, perhaps because Phoenix is a pleasant and easy-to-reach destination but there is also some local loyalty to long-established Spring Training tenants and pre-Diamondbacks favorites.

It helps that the D-Backs won the World Series in 2001 on Luis Gonzalez' walk-off blooper in Game 7 in Phoenix. That came during Randy Johnson's run of four consecutive Cy Young Awards that made him a hero in Arizona. Outsize caricatures of both Johnson and Gonzalez take part in the fifth-inning Legends Race.

The park was initially called Bank One Ballpark, and is still affectionately known as 'The BOB' for short, despite the official name change in 2004.

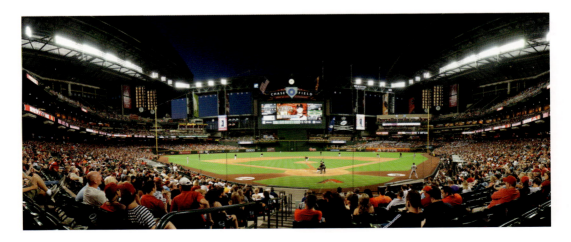

'The Battery'

Truist Park

Cumberland, GA

The Braves have previously abandoned both Boston and Milwaukee, but it was still a shock when they left Atlanta in 2017. Except they didn't really – their new park is in Cumberland, Cobb County (named for a 19th century politician, not the Georgia Peach, Ty Cobb), and it still technically counts as Atlanta. Just.

The Braves' residency at Turner Field, the retrofitted 1996 Olympic Stadium, lasted only 20 years. It needed expensive renovations and, although located in a downtown area, it did not benefit from the kind of social ambience found around Coors and Petco. The move to the affluent Northern suburbs still presents a traffic issue but it does take the team closer to its perceived fan base demographic.

One of the main incentives to move was the opportunity to benefit from associated real estate development. 'The Battery Atlanta' complex around the stadium includes bars and restaurants, apartments, hotels and major corporate offices, and is already established as a signature year-round destination. The fans certainly seem to love it and this model may be the blueprint for the next generation of sports stadia.

The actual ballpark is nice, if somewhat generic, although it does have a zip-line and climbing wall. On-field excitement comes from the 'Beat the Freeze' handicap sprint race, and of course, the Braves won the World Series in 2021. The team have locked in most of their young talent on long-term contracts which makes it more likely that fans will invest in a jersey with a player's name on it, although perhaps it will be the team's contentious name on the front that eventually changes?

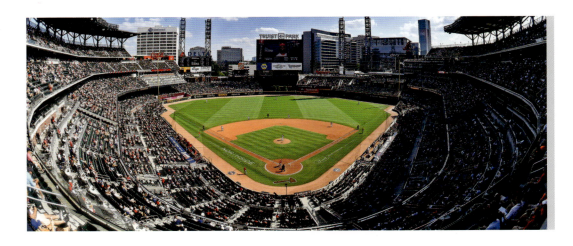

'The Park That Changed Baseball'

Oriole Park at Camden Yards

Baltimore, MD

The opening of Camden Yards on 6 April 1992 changed the narrative on ballpark design and brought about the end of the multi-sport 'cookie-cutter' stadium era. It inspired a wave of demand for compact urban parks created specifically for baseball and within 25 years, over two-thirds of MLB clubs had built new stadiums.

The new Oriole Park was always likely to be a baseball-only facility after the NFL Colts' midnight flit to Indianapolis in 1984 left the O's as the only team in town. The Baltimore & Ohio Railroad site at Camden Yards on the edge of the Inner Harbor area offered a great urban location and provided the park's signature feature: the massive red-brick B&O Warehouse. The iconic renovated warehouse and the pedestrianized Eutaw Street in front of it adjoin the actual stadium bowl and provide an integrated and fan-friendly experience with popular eateries like ex-Oriole slugger Boog Powell's famous BBQ stand.

The new stadium itself mirrored the red brick and arches of the warehouse and took inspiration from the revered 'jewel box' parks of an earlier era by using traditional features to create a retro style - but with better sight-lines, modern amenities and comfort. Many other detailed and stylish features were built in, such as the classical clock which sits atop the scoreboard, reflecting the style of the nearby Bromo Seltzer Arts Tower which was once easily visible from the park before new high-rise buildings closed in.

The new stadium was christened with the compromise name of 'Oriole Park at Camden Yards' and became the first sports venue to win a major design award from the American Institute of Architects. The Baltimore fanbase also warmly embraced the new 'old' look and they flocked to the new venue in record numbers.

The first great moment under the lights atop the Warehouse came on

6 September 1995. When that night's long-anticipated game became 'official' in the middle of the fifth-inning, millions were watching on TV as Cal Ripken Jr.'s 2,131st consecutive game trumped the revered record of Lou Gehrig to make the beloved Oriole shortstop baseball's new 'Iron Man'.

Unbelievably, the next great moment came exactly one year later with Eddie Murray's 500th home run; a feat commemorated with the installation of an orange seat in right-center field to mark the spot. Another orange seat marking one of Ripken's record-breaking homers had to be relocated after the left-field fences were lowered and moved in for the 2022 season in an effort to make the field more equitable for pitchers.

Murray and Ripken are among the Baltimore greats honored with statues at the park but most of the attention focuses on Babe Ruth, who did not actually play for the Orioles at major league level but grew up on the very edge of Camden Yards. That former home has been adapted as a museum in his honor and the 'Babe's Dream' statue stands at the gates to Eutaw Street, with pedants quick to point out that the real Babe was left-handed but the statue is carrying a right-handed glove.

Eutaw Street is a popular landing place for long-balls and each one is marked with a baseball-shaped marker in the ground. It seems likely that the majority of these commemorate hits for visiting players though, as the Orioles' have toiled through endless team-rebuilding phases and have yet to play a World Series game in Camden Yards. The most celebrated home victory of recent years came in September 2011 when a heroic last-game comeback win achieved nothing for the Orioles other than the satisfaction of knocking the rival Red Sox out of the playoffs.

Attendance figures have inevitably dipped from the euphoric highs of the early years, particularly after the Washington Nationals returned to the region, and actually reached zero on 29 April 2015 with rioting on the city's streets leading to a closed-doors game. Orioles' fans still attend in good numbers though and their loud emphasis on the 'O' that starts the seventh line of the Star-Spangled Banner is an enduring tradition and seems appropriate, as the original poem was inspired by the flag over Fort McHenry in nearby Chesapeake Bay in 1814.

Various renovations over the years have helped to maintain the delicate balance between tradition and modern spectator demands and Camden Yards remains one of the most revered parks in the country. Even if its lustre eventually fades, it will always be 'The Park That Changed Baseball'.

'America's Most Beloved Ball Park'

Fenway Park
Boston, MA

Baseball's oldest and most-recognizable ballpark opened on 20 April 1912, six days after RMS Titanic sank and just months after New Mexico and Arizona joined the Union. It pre-dates World War One and is older than iconic US landmarks such as the Empire State Building, the Hoover Dam, the carvings on Mount Rushmore and all but a handful of living Americans.

Esteemed writer, John Updike, once described Fenway Park as "a lyric little bandbox of a ballpark", noting that "everything is painted green and seems in curiously sharp focus". Despite its advancing years and several modernizations, those words still ring true today and the always-immaculate park continues to resonate as a living museum for a bygone age of America's favourite pastime.

Of course, the grand old ballpark is not without its flaws and has always been restricted by its size and shape, dictated by the layout of the surrounding streets in Boston's Back Bay Fens. The geometry of the wildly asymmetric outfield fence presents a challenging conundrum, especially the oddly-angled area adjacent to the bullpens known as 'The Triangle' which has made a fool of many visiting fielders over the years - most notably Torii Hunter in a 2013 ALCS game.

The park also has very narrow foul territory and notably short distances down both the right and left field lines. In rightfield, the 'Pesky Pole' is only 302 feet from home plate; the shortest outfield distance in Major League Baseball. It is named for the light-hitting all-star shortstop Johnny Pesky who sneaked most of his six career homers at Fenway over the fence in that corner.

In leftfield, a 37-foot plastic-coated wall known as 'The Green Monster' is all that stops balls flying out of the park onto Lansdowne Street with excessive

regularity. The incongruous sight and sound of a ball clunking high off what is akin to a giant pinball bumper, as fielders attempt to guess the angle of carom, can add an element of farce to America's favorite pastime. In some respects, it can be seen as out of place in this glorious ballpark, yet it is undoubtedly one of the most iconic stadium features in all of sport.

The Red Sox won the World Series in their first year at their new ballpark and added another three titles by 1918, although two of those series were played at Braves Field, as Fenway offered insufficient capacity. The Sox's fortunes changed for the worse in 1920 after Babe Ruth was sold to the Yankees, allegedly to fund the musical 'No, No Nanette'. This invoked "The Curse of the Bambino" which saw the Yankees deliver 26 world championships before the title finally returned to Boston, despite the best efforts of legends such as baseball's most splendid hitter: Ted Williams. A single red seat in the bleachers marks his 502-foot home run in 1946: the longest in Fenway's history. Williams, Pesky, Dom DiMaggio and Bobby Doerr feature in the revered "Teammates" statue outside Gate B at Fenway, commemorating one of many fine but cursed Red Sox rosters and their life-long friendship.

It took 86 years, but good times never seemed so good for Sox fans as when the curse-busting team of 2004 finally won the World Series for Boston. Three more championships followed over the next 14 years, most notably the emotional 2013 'Boston Strong' win. Each April, Fenway hosts a morning game on Patriots Day as runners in the Boston Marathon pass the ballpark, so the bomb attack on that year's race was literally too close to home for Red Sox Nation. Before the following home game, revered Dominican slugger David Ortiz provided one of Fenway's most evocative moments with his "this is our f***ing city" speech and the bond between Boston and its ballclub had never been stronger.

The club's traditional eighth inning song, 'Sweet Caroline', was reportedly written by Neil Diamond for JFK's daughter, Caroline Bouvier Kennedy. 100 years after her great-grandfather, Mayor John F. Fitzgerald, threw out the ceremonial first pitch at Fenway's inaugural game, it was Sweet Caroline herself who did the same at the park's centennial celebration in 2012.

Grumblings over limited capacity, lack of spectator comforts and restricted corporate opportunities periodically spark heretical talk of Fenway's possible demise but, after further renovations and its addition to the National Register of Historic Places, it appears that a pilgrimage to the old bandbox will remain top of the bucket-list for ballpark-chasers for many more years to come.

'The Friendly Confines'

Wrigley Field
Chicago, IL

Elwood Blues of The Blues Brothers never actually lived at 1060 West Addison Street in Chicago; it's just a fake address he gave to fool the police, but what we now know as Wrigley Field has been there since 1914. The Cubs moved in two years later and were subsequently bought by chewing gum magnate, William Wrigley Jr., with the ballpark name changed to his in 1926.

The art deco-style marquee which reads "Wrigley Field: Home of Chicago Cubs" was first installed at the main entrance in 1934 and settled into its current iconic wording and color scheme by 1960. An LED strip-sign was added to it in the early '80s and famously displayed a "Save Ferris" message for the 1986 movie 'Ferris Bueller's Day Off'.

The vines for Wrigley's ivy-covered outfield walls were planted in 1937 and in the early months of the season, it is possible to see the solid brick surface underneath, as the historic park was granted an exemption from MLB's requirement for padded walls. By summer, the ivy has bushed-out and any baseball becoming lodged in the foliage results in a ground rule double. An over-hanging chain-link 'basket' fence runs along the top, primarily to stop any of the self-styled 'bleacher bums' falling onto the field.

The manual scoreboard in the bleachers was also installed in 1937 and the clock added in 1941. No player has yet been able to hit the scoreboard, even when the wind is gusting in from Lake Michigan. The winds at Wrigley are wildly unpredictable, which draws a lot of attention to the flags at the park during a game. The retired numbers of Cubs greats are displayed as flags on the foul poles, including two #31s, representing both Ferguson Jenkins and Greg Maddux. The current league standings are displayed above the scoreboard and a further flag is raised after the game to indicate a win or a loss for the Cubs.

Plans to install floodlighting in 1941 were abandoned after the requisite materials were donated to the national war effort. The Cubs played 5,687 consecutive day games at Wrigley before finally installing lighting in 1988; the last team to do so.

Wrigley is often referred to as 'The Friendly Confines' but it's not always been sweetness and light on the North-Side. In 1983, Lee Elia launched a memorable and astonishingly profane, post-match managerial tirade against a section of the club's day-time clientele. Twenty years later, nearly a century of Cubs fans' World Series frustration was unloaded onto one of their own, Steve Bartman, after he interfered with a potentially catchable ball in a vital postseason game.

The "Tinker to Evers to Chance" team had brought world championships to Chicago in 1907 and 1908 but a barren run had already stretched to 1945 before 'The Curse of the Billy Goat' was invoked by a local bar owner named William Sianis, who was apparently incensed by his pet goat being ejected from Wrigley during that year's World Series. The Cubs lost and did not even play in a World Series for the next 71 years until, on the 46th anniversary of Sianis's death, they clinched the 2016 National League pennant, before going on to win the World Series in Cleveland. With that win, even Steve Bartman's personal curse was over and the Cubs' owners presented him with a conciliatory championship ring.

Even in the midst of that tense 2016 World Series, prominent Cubs fan, comedian Bill Murray, lightened the mood by performing the traditional seventh-inning stretch rendition of 'Take Me Out to the Ball Game' in the style of Daffy Duck, adding a comic twist to a Wrigley tradition made famous by Hall of Fame Announcer, Harry Caray, and continued by guest conductors since his death. Another musical favorite, the Cubs' traditional 'Win' song, 'Go Cubs Go' by Steve Goodman, entered the Billboard charts in the weeks after that historic victory.

Major renovations in the last decade have literally secured the park's future, with engineers drilling through sand and water to anchor the creaking foundations in bedrock. A Jumbotron scoreboard and additional outfield signage have been controversial, particularly in view of the park's National Historic Landmark status and the impact on outdoor viewing areas on Wrigleyville's established rooftop bars. Facilities for players, press and spectators have all been improved, but only service animals as defined by federal law are permitted on Wrigley Field property, so while the park just might be the G.O.A.T, it's still a no-go for actual goats.

'Wherever the White Sox Play'

Guaranteed Rate Field

Chicago, IL

In a 2007 episode of The Simpsons, Homer visits Chicago and is shown walking past the iconic entrance marquee of Wrigley Field, and then a featureless stadium whose signage says "Wherever the White Sox Play". Although there are ten miles between the two ballparks, it seems that the South-siders' home will forever be in the shadow of its more celebrated neighbor.

When it opened in 1991, New Comiskey Park, as it was initially known, was actually the first of the new wave of replacement ballparks, but although it was modern, there was not a great deal of flair in its design and definitely nothing retro, so it quickly became 'off-trend' when Camden Yards opened the following year.

The new park was constructed right across from the original Comiskey Park and was clearly a significant upgrade in terms of size, comfort and facilities. The two parks stood side-by-side for a short while and long-term Sox fans will have endured some bitter-sweet moments, enjoying the swanky new park while watching a chunk of their past being torn down. Of course, Sox fans nearly did the job themselves in 1979 when the infamous Disco Demolition Night got badly out of control, and three years previously, fireworks had set the park alight during an Aerosmith / Jeff Beck gig.

A lot of homes and businesses around the park have also been demolished, including McCuddy's Tavern, which Babe Ruth used to frequent, so there's not much of a Wrigleyville vibe in the neighborhood. However, Chicago's elevated subway does go directly to Sox-35th station and the food and drink facilities in the park are good.

A modernized version of Bill Veeck's legendary 1960 'exploding' scoreboard is the main attraction at Guaranteed Rate Field. Seven pinwheels on the roof spin and spell out 'home run' when a Sox player goes yard, and there are fireworks and noise to go with it.

The White Sox got off to a terrible start in their new home, losing 16-0 to Detroit on 18 April 1991. A few days later, Hall of Famer, Frank 'The Big Hurt' Thomas predictably became the first home player to make the scoreboard explode and his prodigious slugging was a highlight of the park's first 15 years. Sadly, injury prevented him from playing in the club's World Series win in 2005 but teammate, Jermaine 'Live and Let' Dye, turned in an MVP performance and two blue seats in the outfield mark where Paul Konerko's Grand Slam and Scott Podsednik's walk-off homer landed in a memorable game 2 of the Series.

That triumph came 86 years after the infamous 'Black Sox' scandal of 1919 and gave the South-siders bragging rights in the Windy City for a decade, as the Cubs were still 'cursed' at that time. A Champions Plaza, featuring a granite and white bronze 'Championship Moments' monument, was built outside Gate 4 to commemorate the achievement.

Another World Series hero, Mark Buehrle, further distinguished himself at the renamed US Cellular Field with a no-hitter in 2007 and a perfect game in 2009. The words "The Catch" appear on the outfield wall where DeWayne Wise made an incredible grab in the ninth-inning to preserve the perfect game.

The park has been significantly modified over the years, most notably in the upper tier which has been reduced in height and the roof extended. The best seats in the house are probably in the Wintrust Scout Lounge behind home plate. They can be accessed by their own entrance, Gate 3 ½.

The Xfinity Kids Zone is an excellent facility with batting cages and a youth-sized diamond where the club offer free coaching and skills instruction. The White Sox mascot, Southpaw, is often found there too. The 'green fuzzy dude' was the 25th inductee into the Mascot Hall of Fame, which is located 14 miles away in Whiting, Indiana. The White Sox also offer first-time visitors a complimentary commemorative certificate.

Following two shocking on-field assaults in 2002 and 2003, only fans with seats in the 100-level can access the main concourse and lower seating area, so patrons from upper levels are not able to watch batting practice close-up.

White Sox fans still get pumped up when the team runs out to 'Thunderstruck' by AC/DC. The club have repeatedly tried to replace it but, more than 40 years after Disco Demolition Night, Sox fans are still willing to fight for their rock and metal music. Peacefully, of course.

'Two Out of Three Ain't Bad'

Great American Ball Park

Cincinnati, OH

At first glance, the name of the park seems a bit immodest but, of course, it's been named by a corporate sponsor. There's an awful lot to like about this 2003 park though. It sits on the banks of the Ohio River, alongside the site of their previous home, Riverfront Stadium, in a redeveloped area that also includes the NFL Bengals' stadium. The riverside location offers a variety of pre- and post-game leisure activities, including the acjacent 'The Banks' entertainment district and there are even more leisure options just across the river in Newport, Kentucky and patrons can cross from there by boat or via the Taylor-Southgate Bridge.

The ballpark itself reflects its location and the team's long history. The outfield is dominated by two huge smokestacks reminiscent of the old steamboats that used to ply their trade on the river. They emit flames when the Reds get a strikeout and launch fireworks for every Reds home run and win. The Reds also have one of the coolest 'Win' songs in baseball; 'Unstoppable' by local glam-rock heroes, Foxy Shazam, and their seventh-inning stretch song is equally good; Connie Smith's 'Cincinnati, Ohio'.

Alongside the smokestacks is a riverboat-shaped bar area and a Toyota Tundra truck which can be won by a fan if a Reds player hits a sign between the smokestacks or the actual truck. It's never been done, but a truck was given away in 2015 and another in 2018 when a Jesse Winker blast came within inches. In 2022, one frustrated fan announced on Reddit that he intended to use the vehicle as a 'dump truck' by defecating in it as a protest at the team's awful performance. He didn't do it! The river is too far to hit a fly-ball into, but in 2004 Adam Dunn launched a 535-feet homer out of the stadium which then bounced another 200 feet into the water and so potentially left the state, as the border begins at the river.

The park was designed with a break in the stands between home plate and third base. 'The Gap' is aligned with Sycamore Street and offers views of the downtown skyline, whilst also facilitating a re-alignment of the left-field seats to a better angle and bringing them closer to the field.

In 2015, GABP became the first MLB park to offer a dedicated Nursing Suite for new mothers. Other parks soon followed but the facilities at Cincinnati are still rated among the best on offer.

The Reds are widely considered to be the first professional baseball team in history and an 1869 Cincinnati team is depicted in 'The First Nine' mosaic at the park. It is located inside the main gates near the Crosley Terrace, which honors the Reds' most beloved former home, Crosley Field. Since 1876, the Reds traditionally host a home game on baseball's opening day of the season and the city marks the occasion with an unofficial local holiday and the Findlay Market Parade.

Another mosaic represents 'The Great Eight'; the core players of Sparky Anderson's 'Big Red Machine' team that dominated baseball in the first half of the seventies, culminating in World Series wins in 1975 and 1976. The most prominent of the eight is Pete Rose, the all-time MLB leader in hits with 4,256. There are many tributes to him around the park, including a Rose Garden and banners depicting his 4,192nd hit which broke Ty Cobb's record. The 14 bats on the smokestacks also represent his playing number. A problematic character, Rose was banned from baseball in 1989 for gambling on games he was involved in for the Reds, and other controversies have swirled around him since.

Despite many appeals, Rose remains ineligible for the Baseball Hall of Fame, but he does feature prominently in the excellent Reds Hall of Fame and Museum, which is widely considered the best in baseball outside of Cooperstown.

Whilst it definitely lives up to two of the three words in its name by being American and a ballpark, for all its charms, GABP has yet to witness a truly successful home team and the kind of great nights which bring a ballpark to life, build associated memories and strengthen emotional ties. After the first 20 years in their new park, the Reds have still to win even a single postseason game at home, but the memories of The Big Red Machine dominating at the inferior Riverfront Stadium still live deep in the hearts and minds of Cincinnatians. Greatness awaits.

'The Jake'

Progressive Field
Cleveland, OH

In November 2016, Progressive Field hosted one of the most unforgettable nights of baseball in recent memory. Despite a dramatic fight back by the home team, the Chicago Cubs' curse-breaking World Series Game 7 win resulted in the unwanted record for the longest World Series drought passing to a Cleveland club. Indeed Cleveland have the longest active World Series win drought, and have not won the World Series championship since 1948.

Jacobs Field, as it was originally named, opened 22 years earlier in April 1994, with President Bill Clinton in attendance to throw out the ceremonial first pitch. Like Camden Yards two years before, the new urban ballpark was designed by HOK Sports with a more modern-retro theme and was widely praised for its functionality and appearance. The park offers views of the downtown Cleveland skyline, and the white steel external structure and distinctive light towers are said to reflect the city's industrial heritage. Sadly, the park's inaugural season came to an early end in August when a players' strike wiped out the rest of the campaign.

Cleveland's lamentable lack of success at their former home, Cleveland Municipal Stadium, was lampooned in the 1989 movie 'Major League' but their on-field fortunes improved considerably in the new park's second year with an appearance in the 1995 World Series. Success in following seasons, including another Fall Classic appearance in 1997, inspired a then-MLB record run of 455 sell-out crowds which only ended in 2001. The club marked the feat by 'retiring' a number 455 jersey bearing the name 'The Fans' and placed it alongside those of legendary former players at the park.

The playing field features asymmetrical fences of varying heights, most notably a high wall in left field known as 'The Little Green Monster'. Other than being perceived as having a slight advantage

in favor of pitchers, the park does not appear to confer any significant home field advantage; perhaps other than "The Bug Game" in 2007 when a swarm of midges from Lake Erie descended on Yankees pitcher Joba Chamberlain and helped swing a crucial playoff game the way of Cleveland.

The naming rights for the park passed to Progressive Corporation in 2008 but the building is still primarily referred to as "The Jake". Subsequently, after years of protest from Native American groups, the Cleveland Indians name was dropped and the club renamed as The Guardians prior to the 2022 season. The news was announced in a video with an iconic voiceover by super-fan Tom Hanks, who also brought 'Wilson' the 'Cast Away' volleyball with him when throwing out the first pitch on Opening Day 2022. All references to the former name and the 'Chief Wahoo' caricature were removed from the stadium and fans are now prohibited from entering the stadium if wearing the once traditional war-paint and tribal head-dresses.

The new name was derived from 'The Guardians of Traffic'; eight distinctive art-deco statues that have stood near the site of Progressive Field since the 1930s. They are located on the Hope Memorial Bridge which brings traffic over the Cuyahoga River and leads right up to the stadium gates. The bridge itself was renamed in 1983 for Harry Hope, one of the stonemasons who worked on the Guardians statues, and is also said to honor his co-workers and his son, entertainer Bob Hope, who was raised near the city.

Further modern amenities have been added to The Jake over the years including the distinctive glass-fronted Terrace restaurant in left field. Solar panels were installed in 2007 and they even briefly experimented with a wind turbine in 2012. The park underwent significant renovations between 2014 and 2016. These were particularly focused on opening up the right field district and relocating the bullpens to a raised location in the outfield, making the relief pitchers' warmups easily visible to fans.

As well as statues for legendary players like Bob Feller, Larry Doby and Jim Thome, the outfield also contains Heritage Park, an area behind the center-field tree line accommodating plaques honoring iconic Cleveland players. The club also plan to install a brass replica of the drum used by much-loved fan John Adams, whose tribal beats were a recognizable soundtrack at The Jake and the former Cleveland Stadium for over 50 years. A gold plaque was also placed on John's seat high in the left-centerfield bleachers.

Of course, you can be sure that there will definitely still be space among the Heritage Park monuments to honor members of any future Guardians team which can finally end that World Series drought for the city of Cleveland.

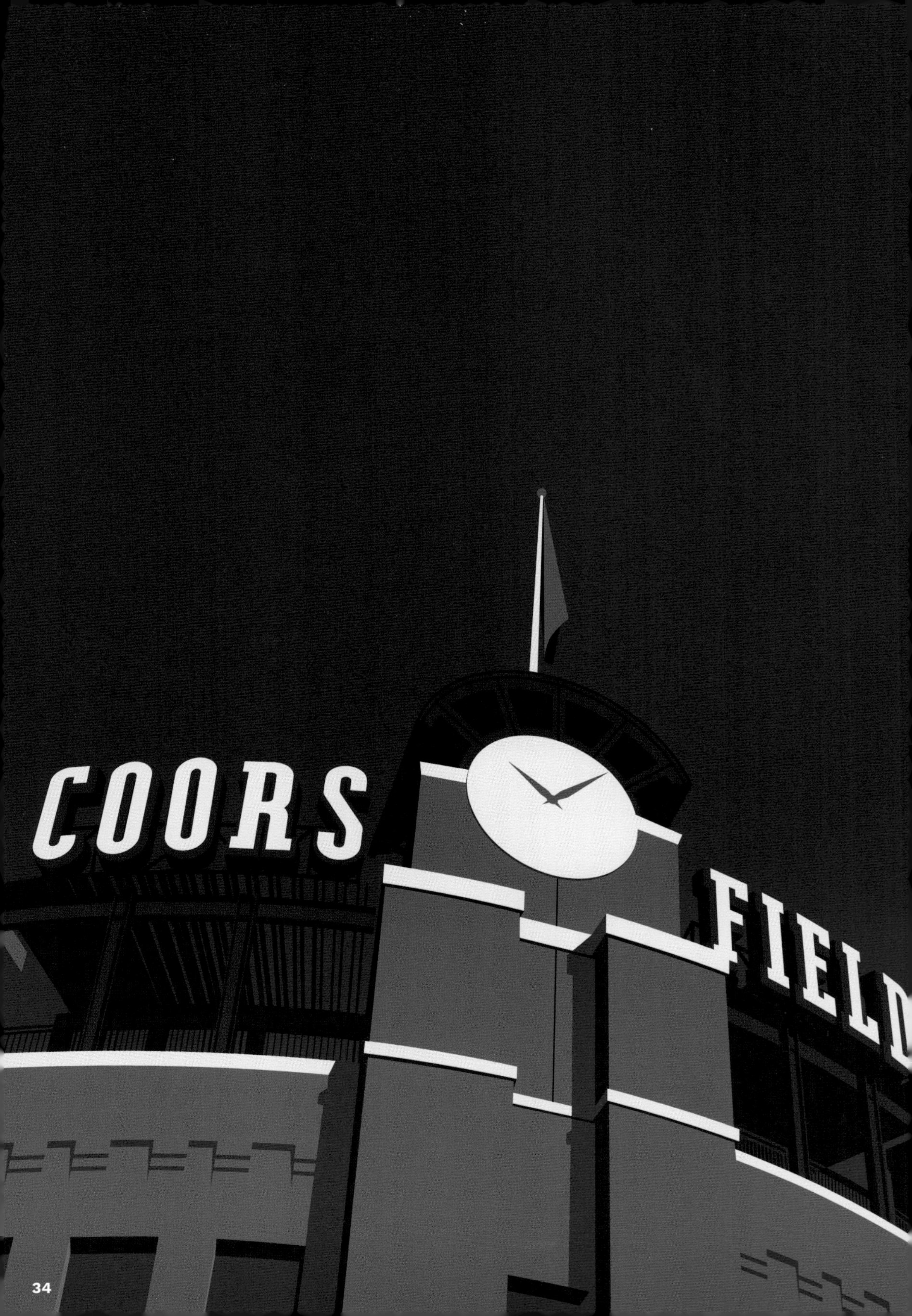
COORS
FIELD

'Rocky Mountain High'

Coors Field

Denver, CO

Some folks still think of the Colorado Rockies as the 'new boys', but, surprisingly, Coors Field is the third oldest ballpark in the National League, having opened in April 1995. The club were an expansion team in 1993 and are actually the second team to bear that name; the first being an NHL team that left Denver to become the New Jersey Devils in 1982. For their first two years, the Rockies played at the Broncos' Mile High Stadium and set the MLB season-attendance record of nearly 4.5 million in year one there.

The new ballpark is the cornerstone of the very successful urban regeneration project which brought the dilapidated LoDo area back to life in spectacular fashion. A similar rejuvenation of nearby Union Station has brought light-rail to the area and it's now quite the hipster enclave. The Rockies later got involved in a real estate side-project of their own: the mixed-use McGregor Square development, which is popular with fans on gameday and features several bars and an outdoor plaza.

The architects adopted a retro style for the park, using red brick and sandstone in order to fit in with the historical warehouse buildings, and a clocktower rotunda provides a classical touch. Forest green steelwork adds a modern aspect and liberal use of columbines, the state flower, on pilasters and sidewalk murals adds a regional flavor. One old building, a 1913 five-story warehouse, has been incorporated into the park as The SandLot micro-brewery, and it was here that the popular Blue Moon beer was first brewed.

The park has the second-highest capacity in the league, after Dodger Stadium, other than the infrequent occasions when the A's open their outfield football stand, but it still provides an intimate spectator experience. The three-tier stand extends right around

the right foul pole and a purple row of seats marks the 'mile-high' point. The top deck in right-field has been converted to The Rooftop terrace, which is one of the areas which offers a distant view of the Front Range of the Rocky Mountains and occasional stunning sunsets.

Rockies fans are very proud of those mountains. Joe Walsh's 'Rocky Mountain Way' is their 'win' song and fans loudly cheer the word 'mountains' when 'God Bless America' is performed, although their favourite shout-along word seems to be 'Tonight' from Charlie Blackmon's walk-up song 'Your Love' by The Outfield. No John Denver though – surprisingly, that's a Baltimore seventh-inning thing. Rocky Mountain Oysters are available at the park but seafood lovers should be aware that these are actually fried bull's testicles. There is a small touch of the mountains inside the park too, where they have built a waterfall feature using real local trees and boulders, and seven fountains shoot water into the air for home runs and wins.

As a result of the altitude and thin air, Coors Field is an absolute nightmare for pitchers, with fly-balls estimated to travel ten per cent further than at sea level. Consequently, the team were early adopters of humidor technology for baseballs and the fences have been pushed out as far as possible. An elevated bleacher section known as 'The Rockpile' was a late addition to center-field and, starting at around 480 feet, it is about as far from home plate as the center-field fence at New York's Polo Grounds was, but tickets are only $4.

After 30 years, the Rockies have still only made five postseason appearances, and always as a Wild Card. In 2007, they beat San Diego in a 'Game 163' tie-breaker after a sensational late-season surge, and went all the way to the World Series before being swept by Boston.

The club have retired the numbers of Todd Helton and Hall of Famer, Larry Walker, but the only player statue outside the ballpark is a generic one, bearing a quote from Branch Rickey: "It is not the honor that you take with you but the heritage that you leave behind."

The fantastic National Ballpark Museum is right across the street. It houses a wonderful collection of memorabilia, including a Denver feature, but with a particular focus on 14 classic ballparks, of which only Wrigley and Fenway survive.

In San Francisco, Pac-Bell / SBC / AT&T Park had so many name-changes that some people simply referred to it as 'Telephone Park'. That shouldn't happen here as brewers, Molson Coors, hold the naming rights in perpetuity. The Rockies' lease with the city runs until at least 2047, so there is still plenty of time for the team to make some history.

'Comerica National Park'

Comerica Park
Detroit, MI

If you didn't know the name of Detroit's ballclub, you would be able to guess it once you got to Comerica Park because there are tigers everywhere at the stadium. The big one outside the main entrance is 15 feet tall and there are half-a-dozen more of them perched around the park's perimeter, plus over 30 tiger heads built into the walls: they've got baseballs in their mouths and there are also claw-scratch marks in the stone.

Once inside, there is a carousel for kids featuring, naturally, 30 tigers; although the nearby Ferris wheel cars are baseball shaped rather than big cats. There are two more tigers atop the giant scoreboard in left-centerfield too, which growl and their eyes light up when the local team hit a home run.

Comerica Park opened in downtown Detroit in 2000 to replace their much-loved but obsolete former home at Tiger Stadium. Two years later, the NFL's Lions moved in right next door and the revitalized area is now known as The District. This incorporates the legendary Fox Theatre and the new arena shared by the Pistons and Red Wings. The park offers a splendid view of the Detroit skyline behind the outfield, most notably the Romanesque Detroit Athletic Club building which dominates centerfield. Right in front of that is the ivy-covered batter's eye and the Chevrolet Fountain which provides spectacular Bellagio-style 'liquid fireworks' displays using water, lights and music.

The team's long history is honored in many ways. The classic old-English 'D' logo still features prominently on the uniforms and is stenciled onto the pitcher's mound before every game. In another nod to tradition, a 'keyhole-style' dirt strip runs from the mound to home plate, which itself is distinctively 'home plate-shaped' rather than round. It is also believed

that a ball signed by the 1999 team was buried below the home plate during the move from Tiger Stadium.

The presentation teams at Comerica are spoilt for choice when it comes to music. As well as anything from the Motown catalogue, popular songs include 'Detroit Rock City' by KISS, 'Eye of the Tiger' by Survivor and Journey's ubiquitous 'Don't Stop Believin'' featuring the line "born and raised in South Detroit", even though no part of the city is generally referred to in that way.

There are few complaints from spectators about the HOK / Populous-designed park which provides modern facilities but has been infused with historical reverence such as the 'decade bats' placed in the main concourse, displaying artefacts from each era of Tiger history. The players have been less satisfied at times though. In particular, the wide-open spaces of the outfield are more conducive to triples rather than homers, leading to regular criticism from home sluggers. In the park's inaugural season, a frustrated Bobby Higginson sarcastically referred to it as 'Comerica National Park' after a shot which would have been a homer in most other parks fell short of the fence. The left-centerfield fence was moved in prior to the 2003 season, which didn't help that year's Tigers, who slumped to an AL-record 119 losses, but latterly it has been useful to right-handed hitting Miguel Cabrera who notched his 3,000th hit in 2022. Miggy had landed his 500th homer the previous year and his multiple batting titles, MVP seasons and a triple crown make him the most likely Comerica-era Tiger to land a statue in the outfield concourse alongside Ty Cobb, Al Kaline and other legends.

Perhaps surprisingly, the only Tigers pitcher to record a no-hitter at Comerica is Justin Verlander in 2007, although that effort is almost forgotten in comparison to 'The Imperfect Game' that followed in 2010 when the 27th and final out of Armando Galarraga's blemish-free pitching gem was ruined by a blown call of 'safe' at first base by umpire Jim Joyce. The exemplary conduct and sportsmanship of both gentlemen after the game drew widespread praise and earned Galarraga a Medal of Reasonableness and a Chevrolet Corvette but, despite many appeals and a proclamation by the Governor of Michigan, the call was never retrospectively overturned.

In January 2023, the club announced that the center-field fence would be brought in by ten feet and the right-centerfield fence reduced in height from 13 feet to seven feet. It seems that Comerica's National Park status may have been revoked.

'The Juice Box'

Minute Maid Park

Houston, TX

Nowhere symbolizes the turn-of-the-century transition from the out-of-town super-stadium era to the new urban-retro ballpark revolution more starkly than Houston. The still-standing Astrodome was 'the Elvis' of enormo-domes. Sitting like a giant space ship in the middle of a humongous parking lot it seemed so big that it might have had its own zip code and gravitational pull! They called it 'The Eighth Wonder of the World' and it gave its name to AstroTurf and the ball-club that played there, but the three million fans who enjoyed Enron Field's inaugural season in 2000 will not have missed it that much.

The new building's exterior design (theme) was derived from the old Union Station railroad building, which was renovated and incorporated into the new park as a stunning main entrance and team store. Extending the locomotive theme, a replica 1860's steam engine is a signature feature inside the park and it makes a run high above the stands whenever the Astros take the field, hit a home run or win a game.

The park also features a fully retractable roof which, when opened completely, reveals a larger open area than any other comparable stadium. The west wall of the roof contains 50,000 square feet of glass and so provides fans with a view of the city's skyline, even when the roof is closed.

'Ballpark at Union Station' was the working title of the park, but by the time it opened, Enron had bagged the naming rights. After that firm's "Houston, we have a problem" moment, the rights passed to Minute Maid in 2002 and the logs in the train's tender were replaced with oranges shortly afterwards. The park's outfield foul markers were also rebranded in 2006 as "Eat Mor Fowl" poles in a Chick-fil-A sponsorship deal that provides free chicken sandwiches for all patrons when an Astros player homers off one of the poles.

There used to be another pole that players could literally hit in centre-field; an on-field flag pole, apparently in homage to historic in-play poles at Tiger Stadium and old Yankee Stadium. The pole sat atop a steep incline in the outfield playing surface known as 'Tal's Hill', which might have been the second-most famous grassy knoll in Texas in its day. Crosley Field in Cincinnati had featured a natural hill and 'Duffy's Cliff' used to sit in front of what is now known as the Green Monster at Fenway, but you can't risk modern-day $300m players on a hilly obstacle course, so both slope and pole were eliminated when the fences were brought in after the 2015 season.

Most of the park's distinctive features are in left-field. The elevated Crawford Boxes are a rowdy seating area atop the high wall which protects the short left-field line. The wall is green, but not monstrous, and houses the out-of-town scoreboard. The train runs above there and alongside is the Phillips 66 Home Run porch, featuring a vintage gasoline pump which displays a running tally of home runs by Astros since the hitter-friendly park opened.

The team's performance on the field has had more ups-and-downs than the Runaway Train ride at Disney. The Astros brought the first-ever World Series game in Texas to the park in 2005 but were swept by the White Sox. The club's fortunes then tanked, reaching an all-time low in their first American League season in 2013 with a 51-111 record. That performance 'earned' them the first overall pick in the draft for an unprecedented third year in a row and a rare haul of talent acquired around this period set up a dynastic team which reached four World Series in six years, with wins in 2017 and 2022.

That franchise-first win in 2017 was especially poignant for Astros fans after the area was devastated by Hurricane Harvey during the season, even forcing a 'home' series against the rival Texas Rangers to be played in Tampa Bay's Tropicana Field. The postseason renditions of 'Deep in the Heart of Texas' during the seventh-inning stretch were emotional and, despite nationwide vilification after subsequent revelations of sign-stealing, that group of players will always be heroes in Space City and there were no blemishes on the dominant 2022 team.

There are lovely double-play statues of long-time team-mates Jeff Bagwell and Craig Biggio in The Plaza at Minute Maid Park where Astros greats are commemorated and celebrated. It surely won't be long before likenesses of Altuve, Bregman and others from this era join them. Probably no trash cans though.

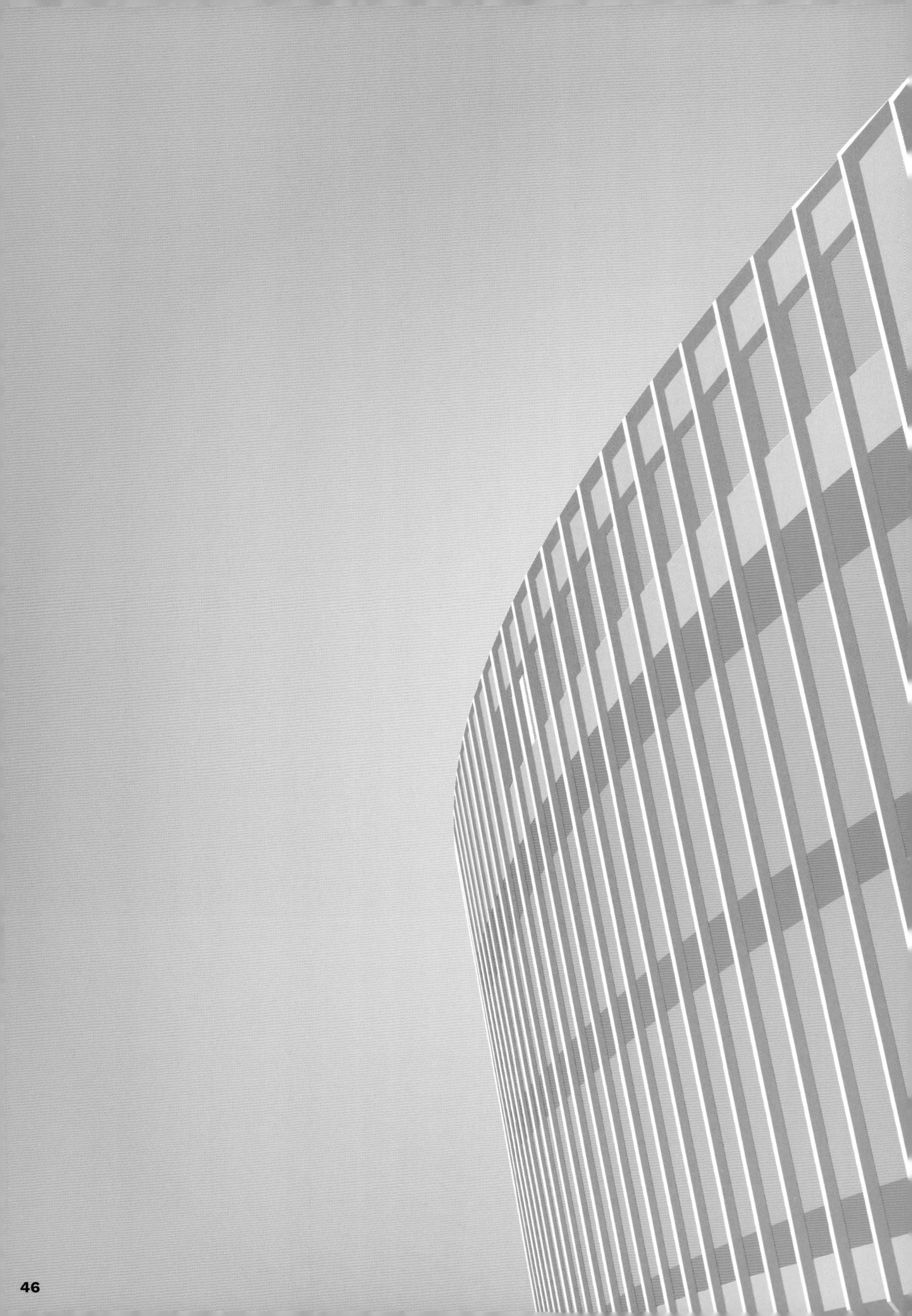

'The K'

Kauffman Stadium

Kansas City, MO

Is the clock ticking down for the league's sixth oldest park? In November 2022, the current owner declared his intention to build a new ballpark in downtown Kansas City, despite a current lease which runs until 2031. The proposal got a mixed response, as there still seems to be a lot of love for 'The K', but it is also clear that the next big trend in baseball is to copy the Atlanta Braves' model and surround a new ballpark with year-round, revenue-generating real estate.

The K seemed futuristic when it opened in 1973. It is located about five miles out of town in the Truman Sports Complex, but crucially, baseball and football got a stadium each, rather than having to share a monster. Kauffman's smooth-flowing lines and curvaceous stands have aged well and when the park was upgraded and future-proofed in 2009, sleek new glass structures were added to improve the exterior aesthetic.

The jewel in the crown was always the outfield area, with its grass embankments, fountains and distinctive crown-topped video board. The grass was a casualty of the Outfield Experience renovations; replaced by much-needed modern amenities, including standing areas, BBQ Pit, the Miller Lite Fountain Bar and the Pepsi Party Porch. The slightly-altered fountains are still spectacular and the replacement Crown Vision display screen really stands out.

Statues of 1985 World Series royalty, George Brett and Frank White, hold court in the outfield. The Royals won again in 2015, but have done little since. Signs of improvement on the field may be important if the team hopes to persuade fans to support public funding for a new ballpark.

'The Big A'

Angel Stadium

Anaheim, CA

The Los Angeles Angels name actually goes all the way back to 1892. In 1961, the new major league team took over the name from the Cubs' Pacific Coast league team and played out of Wrigley Field (not that one – it was located in South Central Los Angeles).

After a stint in Chavez Ravine, they landed in their current stadium beside Disneyland in Anaheim in 1966, making it the fourth oldest stadium in the majors. It was built up and closed-in to accommodate the NFL's Rams in 1980 but was re-configured exclusively for baseball in 1998.

The stadium's defining feature was the giant A-shaped scoreboard which is now in the parking lot, although the halo at the top is still illuminated to signify an Angels win. More recently, the park is best known for the two outsized team caps at the entrance and the artificial rockpile and waterfall in the outfield.

The team was once owned by Disney and was portrayed in the 1994 movie, 'Angels in the Outfield', although when the Angels actually did win the World Series in 2002, their success was credited to the appearance of Rally Monkey – the unofficial mascot of the Angels - during the seventh-inning stretch of Game 6, rather than divine intervention.

A deal had been in place for the current owner to buy the stadium and surrounding land, with plans for major renovations. That would have required a commitment to remain in Anaheim until at least 2050, with an option to stay until 2065, by which time the stadium would be nearly 100 years old. The deal fell through, at least temporarily, in 2022, so the future remains uncertain.

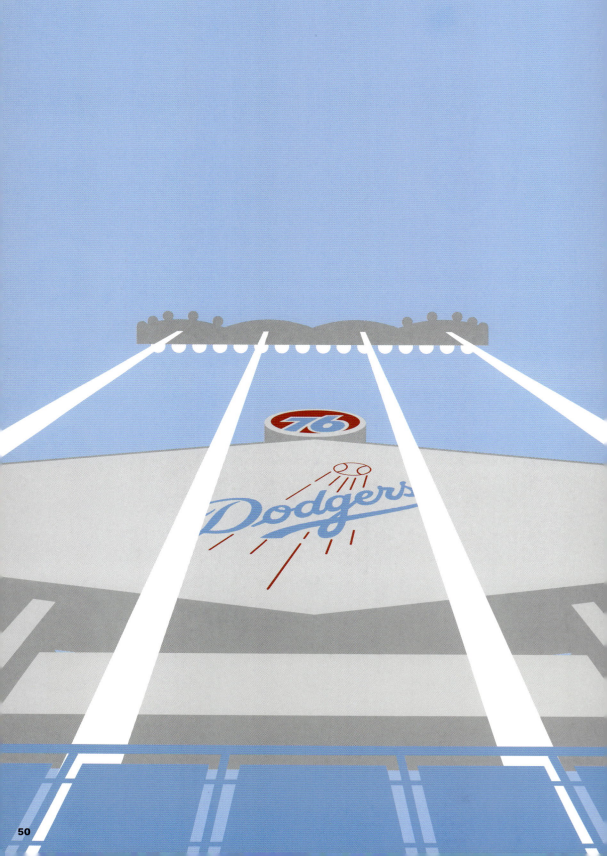

'Blue Heaven on Earth'

Dodger Stadium
Los Angeles, CA

For fans left behind in Brooklyn, Dodger Stadium must have looked impossibly exotic on TV, especially aerial shots, with the bright Californian sun shining down on palm trees, acres of space, the Downtown LA skyline, the San Gabriel Mountains and that immaculate playing field.

The former Brooklyn Trolley Dodgers arrived in Los Angeles in 1958 and had already won a World Series at the not-suitable-for-baseball Los Angeles Memorial Coliseum before Dodger Stadium opened in 1962. The Angels shared the ballpark for its first four years, although they chose to refer to it as Chavez Ravine Stadium and their attendances were low. Years later, the hilarious baseball scene in the first 'Naked Gun' movie was filmed at Dodger Stadium, although the home team was portrayed as the California Angels.

Even after 60 years and many renovations, the stadium still looks as good as it did the first time that Vin Scully announced "it's time for Dodger baseball" there. It now holds an MLB-high 56,000 spectators, with seats in different pastel shades for each of the four levels; starting with yellow at field level and moving up through light orange, sea-green and finally blue for the vertiginous top deck from where you can see it all. Behind the symmetrical outfield fence, the wavy-roofed bleachers and two subtly-proportioned hexagonal video screens have been kept at a discreet level to preserve the view over the mountains.

Dodger Stadium is repainted every year and the club employ an arborist to maintain its extensive native plant collection, which can be viewed on a Botanic Gardens Tour. For food fans, the famous Dodger Dogs are still available on all levels - and they've now added a plant-based version too.

The team's immaculate uniforms remain timeless and classically fashionable, retaining the same

simple logo on a crisp white jersey, topped off by a cap in trademark Dodger Blue with an interlocking LA.

The expansive playing field and benign climate make the stadium something of a pitcher's park. Giant baseballs on the Reserve Level commemorate the eight Dodgers who have won an MLB-best 12 Cy Young Awards – Sandy Koufax and Clayton Kershaw have three each. Kershaw has one of the 13 no-hitters at the park, while Koufax has three, including a perfect game in 1965. Koufax also won four World Series as a Dodger and is now commemorated in one of only two statues at Dodger Stadium, alongside his former team-mate, Jackie Robinson.

In 1981, Mexican pitcher, Fernando Valenzuela, sparked Fernando-mania across the city by winning his first eight games, Rookie of the Year, a Cy Young and the World Series.

Memorable hits at the stadium include two sensational World Series walk-off home runs. In 2018, Max Muncy's dinger against the Red Sox in the 18th-inning ended the longest game in World Series history after more than seven hours. A crippled Kirk Gibson's 'impossible' last-roll-of-the-dice effort in Game 1 of the 1988 Series came after the Dodgers were down to their final strike and they went on to win that series over state-rivals Oakland.

Overall, the Dodgers have won seven World Championships, although their first at Dodger Stadium in 1963 is the only one they have clinched at home. Their most recent success in 2020 was played-out in a Covid-restricted 'bubble' in Texas and they still trail their trans-coast rivals, the Giants, who have won eight.

Fan behavior has sometimes been a serious issue at Dodger Stadium and there have been horrific incidents involving Giants and Dodgers fans in both cities in recent years. The Dodgers are also the last team to forfeit a game, after a 1995 contest against the Cardinals was abandoned because the crowd would not stop throwing souvenir give-away baseballs onto the field after some dubious umpiring.

It was long-serving manager, Tommy Lasorda, who described Dodger Stadium as 'Blue Heaven on Earth' and fans continue to flock to the Elysian Park area - where the stadium is situated - in huge numbers. There is a long-standing joke that Dodgers fans usually arrive in the third-inning because of freeway traffic and leave after the seventh to beat the rush. Proposed solutions have included a gondola and a tunnel for driverless electric cars, but so far, the best option is still the free Dodger Stadium Express bus from Union Station.

The Dodgers have probably the most upbeat and cheerful 'win' song in baseball in Randy Newman's 'I Love LA' so it is a shame that all that love has often evaporated by the time the fans escape the parking lot.

'Little Havana'

loanDepot Park

Miami, FL

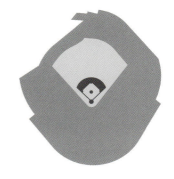

loanDepot Park opened in 2012 – then called Marlins Park – but its bold contemporary architecture and design still make it look like it came from the future. As well as the roof, the glass outfield wall also retracts and offers stunning views of the downtown skyline. Vibrant colors, mosaics and palm trees add to the distinctly Cuban feel but it's the blue glass and curvaceous lines of the bright white building that make it look like a giant spaceship has landed on the former Orange Bowl site in Little Havana.

Location is one reason that the park does not get the attendance and love that it deserves. Maybe building on top of the place where the Hurricanes and the undefeated 1972 Dolphins played is a bit 'Amityville', but traffic and parking are more practical concerns.

Frankly, Miami just does not seem to love the Marlins, despite two World Series wins. Fingers are often pointed at former owners who dismantled those teams and are perceived to have profited from public ballpark funding and frugal payroll, although the speedboat crash which killed José Fernández in 2016 was another blow.

During Derek Jeter's brief tenure as CEO, changes at the park included the closure of the Clevelander nightclub and the removal of the fish tanks behind home plate. The giant pop-art mechanical home run sculpture was also unceremoniously dumped outside the building, as it now sits outside the stadium and was replaced inside the park with social-standing areas.

For now, fans are still staying away, but if the club eventually build another world-class team, perhaps they will come?

'Beer & Sausages'

American Family Field

Milwaukee, WI

They might have changed the stadium's name from Miller Park in 2021 but it's still all about the beer for Milwaukee Brewers fans. And sausages too, but it was the beer that made Milwaukee famous and gave the team its name; they even have 'Roll Out the Barrel' as the seventh-inning stretch song. The team's mascot, Bernie Brewer, definitely likes a brew. After every Brewers home run, he celebrates by sliding down a chute in the outfield, although he no longer lands in a giant glass of beer as he did at former home, Milwaukee County Stadium. For a fee, fans can also slide down the chute after a stadium tour and take a picture with Bernie.

The area's love of sausages and beer probably originates from the state's traditional German and Polish communities. The many sausage-buying options on the concourses can all be sampled with a splash of the famous Secret Stadium Sauce. One of the reasons that the park is seven miles away from downtown is the fans' long-standing love of grilling their own sausages in the parking lot. There's even an annual Arctic Tailgate in late February when fans camp out and party in order to get priority access to single-game tickets.

The Brewers' famous Sausage Race takes place in the middle of the sixth-inning when giant foam-padded sausages race around the warning track. In 2003, Pittsburgh Pirates' first baseman, Randall Simon, caused a pile-up when he playfully whacked the Italian Sausage (actually a petite teenage girl named Mandy) with his bat as the runners came past the away dugout. He was duly arrested after the game, fined and suspended for three games.

Although it sits in a giant parking lot, the park's exterior structure is a pleasingly retro red-brick affair with classical arches and an elegant clock tower. However, that structure is dwarfed by a massive

retractable roof which opens and closes like a fan and allows the seating area to be heated when the Wisconsin weather turns cold. When viewed from outside the main entrance, the roof supports can resemble a Transformers tarantula when closed, but the two sides also form magnificent glass archways with translucent sliding walls below, allowing a tremendous amount of light in.

In common with all the other teams, the Brewers honor franchise legends with a Walk of Fame and a Wall of Honor. The most note-worthy statue is a likeness of broadcaster Bob Uecker sitting in the back row of Section 422, the most distant area of the ballpark, in a comedic call-back to Bob's famous 1970s beer commercials where he was always banished to the nose-bleed seats. The 'Uecker Seats' at Am Fam Park have a restricted view due to the roof supports and are available for around $1.

The most poignant memorial is a bronze public sculpture entitled 'Teamwork', which is dedicated to those who built the park, but in particular, the three ironworkers who sadly lost their lives in 1999 after a massive crane collapsed in high winds.

The roof was closed on April 6 2001 for the park's first Opening Day. President George W. Bush was on hand to throw out one of the ceremonial first pitches but MLB Commissioner Bud Selig took top-billing as a former owner of the team. After the Braves left Milwaukee for Atlanta in 1966, he helped to buy and relocate the bankrupt Seattle Pilots franchise in 1970. He is also credited with safeguarding the club's future after leading a long battle to secure funding for the current ballpark when it looked like the team might have to leave town again.

A particularly beguiling season ticket holder from Oshkosh known as 'Front Row Amy' is perhaps the Brewers' best-known fan. She achieved cult status in 2011 after her meticulous scoring of each game and cleavage-enhancing outfits attracted the attention of TV viewers. Her likeness has appeared on a bobble-head and she now has her own website which promotes the team and displays her 'Brewkini' pictures. In 2019, a local musician named Pete Freeman even released the song 'Front Row Amy' in her honor.

TV's Laverne & Shirley were perhaps the most famous brewery workers in Milwaukee in the '70s, and in 1982 the Brewers nearly made their dreams come true by reaching the World Series. They didn't win, and there haven't been too many 'happy days' since at either park, but they're going to need an awful lot of beer and sausages if the Brew Crew ever manage to win it all in the future.

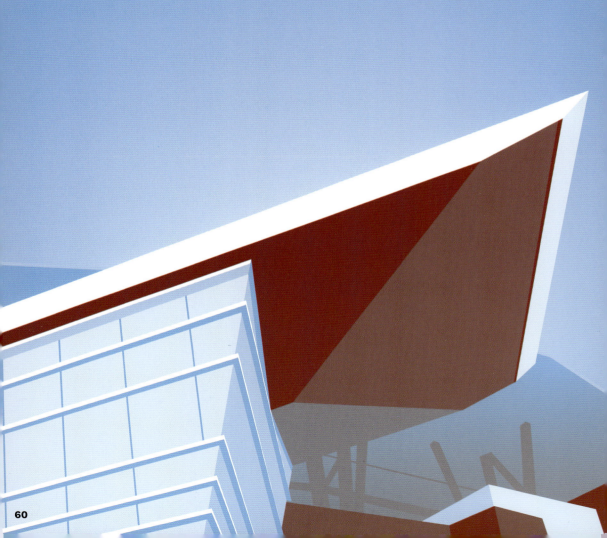

'Minnie-Marvel'

Target Field
Minneapolis, MN

After its first season, Target Field was rated as providing the best stadium experience of any North American major sporting venue in a 2011 poll by ESPN: The Magazine. That's quite an achievement considering the design challenges that architectural design firm Populous and their partners had faced in trying to construct a modern facility on a comparatively small plot of land in the middle of a crowded transport interchange area.

The park is built on an eight-acre site that was formerly a parking lot; a much smaller footprint than any of the other new parks built in the previous 20 years, and is hemmed in by railroad tracks, the I-394 Freeway and other physical limitations. Creative solutions were devised, primarily by building bridges over the roads and tracks to integrate with Target Plaza; a beautifully landscaped two-acre public gathering space and garden which connects the park to the historic Warehouse District of Minneapolis and adds significant space. Target Plaza is open year-round and incorporates the main club store and ticket offices. It acts as the main gateway into the park and also features a giant glove sculpture to honor all the Twins who have won Gold Glove Awards.

The contemporary exterior design of the park is said to represent 'an artistic interpretation of the culture of Minnesotans: a dichotomy of cosmopolitan and natural'. The use of locally-sourced Mankato limestone gives Target Field a distinctly Minnesotan feel. Its attractive golden-hued façade is complemented by extensive use of cantilevered glass and dark brown Brazilian hardwood.

The interior is no-less impressive with fine sightlines and facilities. Flower beds extend around the perimeter of the outfield wall and one small section of seats, known as the 'Overlook', overhangs the right-field warning track and is clad in the same limestone as the park's exterior.

Despite being a similar size to Fenway Park, advances in ballpark design have allowed the club to install a playing field without unnaturally short power alleys or the need for outlandish fencing, although it is still considered a slightly hitter-friendly park. The 2019 Twins set an MLB single-season home run record with 307 dingers.

There is an angular feel to the structural layout, with the designers having to take a creative approach to squeeze all the required facilities in. The impressive Budweiser Roof Deck fits into the left-field corner and offers sweeping views of the downtown Minneapolis skyline, as well as a large fire pit to warm patrons on cool spring evenings. More modern tastes are also catered for; Target was awarded the title of 'best vegan ballpark' in 2018. Truly Hard Seltzer also added their name to the brewpub and deck on the other side of the park, where fans can drink alongside the Twins' two World Series trophies and other memorabilia. Fortunately for imbibing fans, public transportation links to the stadium are outstanding.

The park's most identifiable feature is a 46-feet tall sign portraying the Twins' original "Minnie and Paul" caricature logo which stands high above center-field. It represents unity and the Twins' spirit, depicting two cartoon players wearing the uniforms of minor-league teams from Minneapolis and St. Paul meeting at the Mississippi River that separates the Twin Cities. After a Twins home run, lights flash and the Minnie and Paul figures shake hands. The middle three letters in Twins are highlighted when the home team clinches a win.

Statues of team greats like Kirby Puckett and Rod Carew are displayed in Target Plaza, but following protests over the murder of George Floyd in the city in 2020, a statue of former owner Calvin Griffith was removed because of his widely-known historical racist comments regarding the rationale for relocating the Washington Senators to Minneapolis in 1961. The club has also displayed 'Black Lives Matter' and 'Justice for George Floyd' signage on the outfield fence and a home game against Boston was postponed in 2021 after further civil unrest arising from the death of Daunte Wright resulted in a curfew.

From 1982 – 2009, the Twins shared the Hubert H. Humphrey Metrodome with the Minnesota Vikings football team. That Dome featured a fabric roof, self-supported by air pressure, but was susceptible to deflation during snowstorms and actually fully collapsed in 2010, bringing the NFL Vikings' home schedule to a premature end. With insufficient space on the Target Field site to accommodate a retractable roof, cold weather in October could test fans' resolve, although the team has yet to go deep into the play-offs in their new home and has not actually won a postseason game since 2004.

'King of Queens'

Citi Field

Queens, NY

The Mets have been around for over 60 years now, but they probably wouldn't exist at all if the Brooklyn Dodgers and New York Giants hadn't made their own gold rush to California at the end of the 1950s.

The distinctive brick façade of Citi Field clearly pays homage to the Dodgers' abandoned home park, Ebbets Field, with an eye-catching rotunda as its main entrance, featuring 22 archways and glass panelling which bear a striking resemblance to those once found in Brooklyn. The rotunda's lavish and stunning interior pays tribute to the legendary game-changing Dodger, Jackie Robinson, and exhibits a nine-foot sculpture of his retired #42, as well as pictures and quotes from his life.

Of course, the Mets are more than a Brooklyn Dodgers tribute band and have a storied history of their own, including World Series wins in 1969 and 1986, which are celebrated in The Mets Hall of Fame & Museum. A statue of Tom Seaver, the star pitcher of the 1969 'Miracle Mets', was installed outside the park's main entrance in 2022.

You'll find Citi Field in the Flushing Meadows - Corona Park area of Queens. The Long Island Rail Road and the #7 subway train both stop at Mets-Willets Point Station, which also serves the Billie Jean King National Tennis Center and Arthur Ashe Stadium. A new soccer stadium for New York City FC should also emerge in Willets Point by 2027.

The Mets have their own 'ultras' fan group, 'The 7-Line Army', which takes its name from the subway and the Mets-themed clothing brand which organizes their activities. Once a month, 'the army' books out the Big Apple Reserve Section at Citi Field and also provides vociferous support on specific road trips.

65

The main runway of LaGuardia airport ends just behind the stadium in Flushing Bay, and during a game dozens of planes taking off from there will fly directly over the park at such low altitude that warning lights are required on the lighting towers.

The Mets' former home, Shea Stadium, was dismantled in February 2009, but plaques in the Citi Field parking lot indicate where home plate and all three bases were situated. The original Home Run Apple is also located outside the park. A new Apple, more than four times the size of the old one, has been installed in Citi Field and still pops up to celebrate Mets homers. A new pair of uniquely orange foul poles have also been installed – all other teams use yellow.

Mr Met, one of the most famous mascots in all of sport, has been dishing out high-fours to Mets fans since 1964 and can now be easily found at Fan Fest behind center-field or running the bases with young fans after Sunday afternoon home games.

Citi Field witnessed its first big moment on April 17 2009 when veteran Gary Sheffield clubbed his 500th home run; the first player to hit that milestone wearing a Mets uniform, although he had only signed for the club a few days earlier.

Three months later, Paul McCartney played the first ever concert at Citi Field. The Beatles' 1965 gig is arguably the most famous event to have taken place at Shea Stadium. In a nod to his previous visit to the home of the Mets, McCartney closed out Billy Joel's 'Last Play at Shea' concert in 2008 with 'Let it Be'. The Mets have often played Joel's 'Piano Man' in the middle of the eighth-inning and he is just one of many celebrity fans of the team, including Kevin James, Jerry Seinfeld and Chris Rock. In 2014, Citi witnessed 50 Cent throwing what is widely considered to be the most embarrassing ceremonial first pitch ever; which must make it worse than efforts by Darth Vader, Avril Lavigne, Cookie Monster and virtually every president since William H. Taft.

The 2018 Winter Classic hockey game played at Citi Field was contested by Buffalo and, surprisingly, the New York Rangers, rather than the local Islanders. New York fan allegiances are normally demarcated by the East River, with the newer Mets / Jets / Nets / Islanders fan bases aligned against the more established Yankees / Giants / Knicks / Rangers quartet, although there are many exceptions.

The Yankees may have annexed Jay-Z and 'that' Frank Sinatra song but the Mets have their own signature song; 'Meet the Mets', and also use Ace Frehley's 'New York Groove' as a post-match victory anthem. With the Mets' new owner showing some deep pockets, fans might get used to hearing it more often.

'Across the Street from The House That Ruth Built'

Yankee Stadium

Bronx, NY

Most baseball venues are referred to as 'ballparks', but the Yankees prefer to call their Bronx home a stadium; in fact, THE Stadium. When they closed down the 1923 'House That Ruth Built', they did transport the monuments and trophies across the street, and some of the ghosts probably went along with them too, but at the end of the day, the place where all that history was made is no longer with us.

The current stadium opened in 2009 and is a very good modern facsimile of the old one, albeit bigger, bolder and considerably more expensive. It retains much of the look and feel of the original, especially the imposing granite and limestone exterior, which is reminiscent of the original façade and still features that iconic lettering above the entrance. Once inside, the magnificent seven-story Great Hall concourse is a clear upgrade and the instantly recognizable ornamental frieze that frames the stand roof has been recreated and extended around the entire top deck.

The new playing field has a reputation for home runs, particularly to the short porch in right-field. The opulence of the new stadium and its propensity for luxury suites and corporate seats is perceived to have pushed the more vociferous 'ordinary' fans up to the top tier or the bleachers. According to some players, this has negatively impacted the stadium's noise and intimidation factor, but the 'Bleacher Creatures' can still blow up an occasional ignominious can-throwing storm, alongside their more sedate soccer-style 'roll call' for Yankees' position players.

Monument Park has a new home behind the fence in centerfield. It is hard to believe that the headstone-like monuments to Miller Huggins, Lou Gehrig and Babe Ruth were once in-play on the old stadium's outfield, albeit 461 feet from home plate. After retiring Derek Jeter's #2 in 2017, the Yankees have now retired a total of 23 numbers, including all single-digit numbers other than zero, in a true roll-call of legendary household names.

The Yankees of the new stadium era have started to break previous records and create their own historical moments. In 2022, Aaron Judge's 62nd long-ball of the season broke the unblemished American League single-season home run record set in 1961 by Roger Maris; a lineal record held by a Yankee ever since Babe Ruth set a figure of 60 in 1927.

The most revered modern Yankees dynasty featured the 'Core Four' of Jorge Posada, Mariano Rivera, Derek Jeter and Andy Pettitte, who won four World Series in five years from 1996-2000. They all came through the farm system in 1995 and the first three played together for 17 consecutive seasons, while Pettitte's return helped them bridge the gap to the new stadium, where each one provided more key moments.

The legendary captain, Jeter, struck first, surpassing 'The Pride of the Yankees' Lou Gehrig's all-time Yankee hits record with his 2,722nd on 11 September 2009, before going on to collect his 3,000th hit, a homer, in a memorable five-hit game in front of his home fans in 2011. Legendary closer, Rivera, broke the all-time MLB saves record, also at home in 2011, before making one final 'Enter Sandman' bullpen exit in 2013, and leaving the game for the last time after an emotional mound visit from Pettitte and Jeter. Each of these moments deserves its own place in the hearts and minds of Yankees fans, yet somehow, they still lack the poignancy and finality of Gehrig's "luckiest man on the face of the earth" speech or the dying Babe Ruth's appearance at the second Old-Timers' Day in 1947.

Ultimately, winning means everything to Yankees fans and there's no more quintessentially New York moment than hearing them sing along to Frank Sinatra's 'New York, New York' after a home win (they used to play the Liza Minnelli version of the song when they lost). The original stadium's reverie is rooted in the 26-world championship wins it hosted over 86 years, at an average of 1 every 3.3 years, whilst the Yankees have yet to return to the World Series in the 13 years since winning #27 in their inaugural year at the new stadium.

In time, the new stadium will make its own history, but until then memories of Thurman Munson, Joe Louis vs. Max Schmeling, Wade Boggs on a horse, countless Yogi Berra-isms, George Steinbrenner's 2008 golf cart lap, Pope Paul IV's 'Sermon on the Mound', President George W. Bush's post-9/11 first pitch strike and Mickey Mantle will still live longest in the memory.

'Foul Territory'

Oakland Coliseum

Oakland, CA

Fans at the Oakland Coliseum have witnessed some glorious times, starting with a World Series hat-trick in the early '70s, then the Bash Brothers years and the Goliath-baiting success of the Moneyball era, but sadly, the ageing and decrepit stadium seems to have been in palliative care for some time and is scheduled to close in 2024.

The Coliseum's peak years for baseball were probably in the 1980s after football's Raiders first moved out. Season attendances crept over one million on a regular basis for the first time and hit nearly three million in the year after the Oakland Athletics' 1989 World Series win. The beginning of the end came with the Raiders return and the construction of the giant "Mount Davis" grandstand in 1995, which closed off the stadium and its outfield views.

Not that it was ever a great park; the massive expanse of foul territory in a largely circular stadium makes virtually every pop-up an out and the '60s-built stadium now shows its age with a litany of plumbing, sewage and infestation problems, partly due to the building sitting below sea-level. Attendances dipped below 10,000 a game in 2022 but the A's still drew a one-off crowd of over 56,000 for a Giants game in 2018, with the top-level open.

After the NBA Warriors fled the adjacent Arena for the 'sexier' side of The Bay and the Raiders bailed again, the A's could have the city to themselves if plans for a contentious new waterfront development come to fruition, but, after stints in Philadelphia and Kansas City, a third change of city may still be in their future.

'You Can Ring My Bell'

Citizens Bank Park

Philadelphia, PA

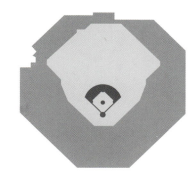

Back in 2004, when most baseball clubs were heading back into the heart of their cities, the Phillies opened their sparkling new park next to their old stadium, out in the South Philadelphia Sports Complex. The city's other sports teams also play out here and there's even a 3,500-seater esports venue on the way for the city's Overwatch League team. However, the ballpark does offer distant views of the city skyline and the complex is well-served by SEPTA trains. Facilities in the area are expanding too, including the $50m Xfinity Live! Center which is basically a mall full of massive sports bars and beer halls instead of shops, which can service an awful lot of sports fans.

Of course, fans of Philly sports teams are often described as 'an awful lot' or worse, partly arising from the 1968 Eagles game when an irate crowd turned on Santa, who was booed and pelted with snowballs. The Phillies and Eagles used to share Veterans Stadium, but they also shared the GQ award for 'worst fans in America' in 2011. The infamous 'intentionally vomiting on an 11-year-old girl' incident in 2010 might have been partly behind that. Fan behaviour has not been a particular concern in the new ballpark, although apparently Phillies relievers had to beg the club to move them to the lower of the two split-level bullpens adjacent to the outfield concourse so that fan abuse would primarily be directed at the visitors, not them.

Even the club's popular mascot, the 'Phillie Phanatic' has been described as the "most-sued mascot in the majors"; although the big green, furry 'thing' has also been voted 'the best mascot in sports' by Forbes and Sports Illustrated and appears in both the Mascot Hall of Fame and the National Baseball Hall of Fame in Cooperstown.

An even more popular figure at the park was long-time play-by-play announcer, the late Harry Kalas. The Phillies still

play a video of him singing 'High Hopes' to celebrate victories and there is a statue in his honor near Ashburn Alley - an outfield plaza and entertainment area named after his friend and broadcast colleague, Richie Ashburn.

As well as statues, other fine art on show at the park includes a giant 'Phillies Dream Scene' oil painting, mosaics and a terrazzo tile floor featuring images of popular Phillies in action.

The exterior architecture is largely comprised of multiple shades of red brick, topped by a green roof with a copper patina finish. Black accent bricks form the shape of baseball diamonds across the top of the three primary façades and the word, "Philadelphia", is spelled out in black bricks along Pattison Avenue.

The positioning and variable height of the outfield wall from dead-center to left-center has created an area known as the 'Angle' on the playing field, which can cause problems for fielders and produce additional drama.

The ballpark's most prominent feature is a 50-foot-tall Neon Liberty Bell, located high in right-center field, which 'rings' after every Phillies home run and victory, with the bell and clapper illuminating and swaying to the sound of a ringing bell.

That bell became a familiar sound in the early years at CBP as a core squad of largely home-grown players such as Jimmy Rollins, Pat Burrell, Ryan Howard and Cole Hamels sparked a golden era for Phillies baseball, culminating in a World Series win in 2008. That triumph inspired the memorable 'World Series Defense' episode of the hit TV series, 'It's Always Sunny in Philadelphia', which featured a goofy fan letter from Rob McElhenney's character, Mac, to All-Star second baseman, Chase Utley.

The deciding Game 5 of that World Series conclusively proved that it is not always sunny in Philadelphia. It began on Monday, October 27, but was suspended in the sixth-inning, with the score tied 2-2; the first ever rain-shortened game or suspension of play in World Series history. Two days later, the game was completed and a Phillies win over Tampa Bay clinched the second world championship in franchise history.

In 2022 the Phillies made it back to the World Series and were again victims of the Philadelphia weather, with Game 3 rained-out. They eventually lost to Houston over six games. Some of the heroes of 2008 were brought back for ceremonial first pitches before home games in that series. Jimmy Rollins threw to 'Whiplash' star, Miles Teller, while Rob McElhenney, now owner of Wrexham AFC, got to fulfil his old TV character's wish by catching a throw from 'his' hero, Chase Utley.

'Take Me to the River'

PNC Park
Pittsburgh, PA

Why are the Pittsburgh Pirates called the Pirates? They just aaarrr! Actually, it's because in 1891, the Pittsburgh Alleghenys ball club were accused of 'pirating' a player away from Philadelphia after exploiting a loophole and the name just stuck.

That original team name was derived from the Allegheny River, which flows through Pittsburgh before joining with the Monongahela River to form the Ohio River: the Three Rivers after which their previous stadium was named. PNC Park is located on the North Side of the Allegheny, with a quite stunning view of the Pittsburgh skyline, the river and the 'Aztec Gold' colored, Roberto Clemente Bridge which spans it. The bridge is pedestrianized on gamedays, or fans can cross by riverboat and there is also a lovely riverwalk to enjoy.

The park itself is a beauty. As it is in Pittsburgh, it naturally makes good use of steel, but also ochre-colored Kasota limestone and smooth stone. Unusually for a modern ballpark, it has only two seating decks and is designed to get all of the fans as close to the action as possible. Crucially, the giant scoreboard and the light towers are set off to the sides, ensuring that, unlike Oracle Park in San Francisco, all the seats in both tiers can enjoy the park's spectacular outlook to the full. The center-field seating is capped at seven rows and the club have been developing patio and bar areas there too. The tallest structure is the batter's eye, which is accessorized by some neat topiary spelling out 'Pirates' in front of it.

Although PNC has a reputation as a pitcher's park, it has only hosted one no-hitter to date. The distance from home plate to the river is 443 feet. By September 2022, only five home runs had splashed into the river on the fly, including two by Josh Bell. Garrett Jones was the first Pirate to do it, narrowly missing a couple riding a tandem bike on the path, and Pedro Álvarez managed to hit one into a boat.

The spirit of Roberto Clemente is everywhere at PNC Park. If not for the financial imperative of selling naming-rights, it would have been named after him and that is what prompted the city to rename the former Sixth Street Bridge in his honor. Clemente spent all of his 18-year career with the Pirates, leading them to two World Series wins and was a 15-time All-Star. In his final season, he won the last of 12 consecutive Gold Gloves and reached 3,000 hits with just two days to spare. He was inducted into the Hall of Fame in 1973; the first Latin American or Caribbean player to be enshrined at Cooperstown.

Clemente's statue sits outside the park near his bridge. 1960 World Series Game 7 walk-off hero Bill Mazeroski also has a statue, as does two-time World Series winner, Willie Stargell, who tragically passed away just hours before the new park opened on 9 April 2001.

Inspired by Barry Bonds and Bobby Bonilla, the Pirates won three straight division titles from 1990 to 1992 but then inevitably lost Bonds to San Francisco and Bonilla to the Mets, who still pay him over $1m every July, even though he retired in 2001. The Pirates subsequently recorded 20 consecutive losing seasons before Andrew McCutchen inspired three glorious playoff runs from 2013-2015, with over 40,000 fans squeezing into PNC for the NL Wild Card Game in 2015.

The Pirates have been very poor since and currently have the longest pennant drought in the National League. Fans have become frustrated with the owner after several seasons of rebuilding and low payroll, not helped by seeing the Steelers and Penguins lift eight world championships between them since the Pirates last ruled the world.

At least fans can still enjoy a scenic day out at the park, perhaps munching on a Primanti Bros sandwich while watching The Great Pierogy Race at the end of the fifth-inning. The Pierogi also compete against Washington's Presidents and Milwaukee's Sausages whenever their teams play each other.

PNC is also one of the parks that hosts golf experience days that allow fans to tee off from the upper deck and land shots on marked 'holes' on the playing surface. The temptation to grip it and rip it into the river must be strong. Happy Gilmore may not be welcome.

'Splash Hits'

Oracle Park

San Francisco, CA

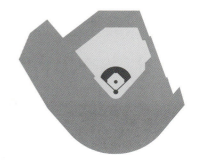

They call the upper tier at Oracle Park the "View Level" for a reason: most seats offer fantastic vistas over the glorious waters of San Francisco Bay, the Bay Bridge and the East Bay Hills on the horizon. The look-out could have been even better, but the planned orientation of the stadium was altered to provide as much shelter as possible from the wind, bearing in mind that a pitcher was once blown off the mound at their former home, Candlestick Park. It's only seven miles down the coast, but the 'Stick had its own micro-climate and foghorn and could be a very inhospitable spot indeed.

The historic China Basin district used to be a no-go area, but is now a thriving cosmopolitan neighbourhood and the ballpark fits right in. Its brick façade mirrors the area's former warehouse buildings and the charcoal-colored steelwork matches the Lefty O'Doul bascule bridge, which connects the site to Mission Bay.

The body of water which sits just beyond the tall right-field wall at the park is known as McCovey Cove and is named after esteemed first baseman, Willie McCovey. A statue of lefty-swinging McCovey stands across the China Basin, and one depicting his revered 1960s team-mate, Willie Mays, is located outside the main entrance.

Home runs hit directly into the water are known as 'Splash Hits'. After 23 seasons, Giants hitters have achieved this feat 97 times, of which 35 were achieved by Barry Bonds, including the first four at the park. Visitors have added 54 such hits, and so far, none have been thrown back by seals, probably because the kayakers who pack the Cove during games get there first.

Giants players' 'Splash Hits' are recorded on an electronic counter on the right-field wall, beside the manual out-of-town scoreboard. The wall has several open arches built into it, through which pedestrians on the

adjacent public walkway can get a free 'knot-hole gang' view of the game for up to three innings each.

The ballpark opened in 2000 as Pacific Bell Park, but it has had about as many name changes as Puff Daddy, with three corporate re-brands over the years. The early years were dominated by Barry Bonds. As the son of Giants legend, Bobby Bonds, and godson of Willie Mays, Barry seemed destined for greatness in orange and black, and he certainly delivered. In 2001, he smashed 73 home runs to set a new single-season record and most of the major milestones in his career home run record chase came in front of San Francisco crowds, culminating on 7 August 2007 with his record-breaking 756th long ball. Bonds went on to set a total of 762 before retiring.

It took more than 50 years for the Giants to claim their first World Series in San Francisco, but in the five seasons between 2010 and 2014, they claimed three, largely on the back of exceptional pitching, with seven pitchers appearing in all three wins. Most of the catching was done by Buster Posey, and 'Kung Fu Panda', Pablo Sandoval, also appeared in all three, including a remarkable three home runs at Oracle in Game 1 of the 2012 Series. Of the core pitching group, Tim Lincecum threw a regular season no-hitter in 2010 and Matt Cain followed up with MLB's 22nd perfect game in 2012.

For 2020, the bullpen mounds were relocated from foul territory to behind the outfield fences, primarily for player-safety reasons. The move also slightly reduced the field's spacious outer dimensions, although the deep right-center area is still renowned as 'Triples Alley'.

The park's outfield area is easily recognizable as a result of the outsized features that dominate left-field. An 80-foot-long Coke bottle lights up with every Giants home run and a massive steel and fiberglass baseball glove sits beside it. There's a decommissioned cable car out there too and the Candlestick foghorn, which sounds for every home win.

San Francisco fans love to join in with a song from Journey during the eighth-inning of a game. That band's singer, Steve Perry, sometimes leads the singing during postseason games. If the Giants are winning, it's 'Lights', but if they're behind, 'Don't Stop Believin'' rallies the crowd, like a Hunter Pence "One More Day With You" speech used to do for the team.

Crowds often hear Tony Bennett's 'I Left My Heart in San Francisco' as they leave the park. Ballpark chasers will also leave a little bit of their own hearts behind after a visit to this wonderful venue.

'Bark at the Park'

Petco Park

San Diego, CA

Petco Park occupies a lovely spot near the San Diego Waterfront, not far from the stunning artwork and statues of the scenic Embarcadero and the USS Midway Museum. Its proximity to the vibrant Gaslamp Quarter also offers excellent accommodation and entertainment options, making it one of the most attractive all-round destinations in baseball.

The park itself features a graceful Indian sandstone and stucco exterior, matching the hues of the locality, while the exposed white steel and extensive use of palm and jacaranda trees fits right in with the breezy SoCal vibe.

Offices, restaurants and concessions are largely housed within several distinctive 'tower' buildings which ring the perimeter. They are separated from the main ballpark structure and seating bowl by a bright and airy concourse, and the two areas are connected by bridges adorned with hanging ivy and cascading gardens of bougainvillea and jasmine plants. Nicely cantilevered grandstands provide excellent sightlines from distinctive dark blue seats and the park also offers a view of the downtown skyline and glimpses of the ocean.

The park opened in 2004, but part of it actually pre-dates Fenway Park. The four-story Western Metal Supply Co. building opened in 1909 and had to be integrated into the new ballpark's design due to its historic landmark status. It houses the team store, bars and rooftop seating, and actually forms part of the outfield boundary, with the southeast corner of the building serving as the left field foul pole: balls that hit the southern wall are foul but those that hit the eastern wall are home runs. Homers onto the roof are rare, but Hunter Renfroe has done it twice and Fernando Tatís Jr. became only the second batter to hit one, in 2020.

Gallagher Square is a grassy park area which sits beyond the outfield, but within the ballpark's gates. It is a popular pre-game picnic spot and does afford a partial view of the playing field and video screens.

As you might expect from its name, Petco Park is the most dog-friendly ballpark in baseball and hosts 'Bark at the Park' themed games and regular pet-adoption days. The popular 'Barkyard' area in the outfield stands provides five semi-private, dog-friendly viewing areas which can accommodate up to four people and two dogs in each. The team store offers a wide selection of player jerseys for dogs, plus bandanas, collars and toys. In addition, Petco's K-9 Promotion offers a free dog toy whenever Padres' pitchers strike out nine or more batters in a game.

The team have also introduced 'The Paw Squad'; three golden retrievers with their own personalized Padres jerseys who act as 'canine ambassadors' on Saturdays. The club also supports the 'Shelter to Soldier' organization which adopts dogs from shelters to train as emotional support animals and psychiatric service dogs for active military personnel, veterans and their families.

With San Diego being home to the Pacific Fleet and several Marine Corps installations, the Padres regularly invite large numbers of military recruits to Petco Park. On Sundays, Memorial Day and other designated 'Military Appreciation' days, the Friars wear distinctive camouflage uniforms instead of their normal brown-and-yellow outfit, and play 'The Marine Hymn' during a fourth-inning stretch to honor their guests.

A statue of long-time radio announcer and former Padres manager, Jerry Coleman is located outside the park and depicts him in Marine aviator flying gear. He saw active service in WWII, before winning four World Series rings as a New York Yankees player, then leaving baseball to serve again in the Korean War. Two further statues, located in Gallagher Square, depict legendary closer, Trevor Hoffman, pitching to eight-time NL batting champion, Tony Gwynn, who is forever revered as 'Mr Padre'.

Before Joe Musgrove's 2021 effort in Texas, the Padres had endured the longest no-hitter drought of any team in MLB history and only Tim Lincecum of the Giants has a no-no at Petco Park. The number of home runs at Petco did increase after 2013 when the fences were moved in, but it is still definitely considered a pitcher's park.

When the NFL's Chargers left for LA in 2017, San Diego became one of the few cities where baseball is the only major league sport in town. The Friars have won National League pennants in 1984 and 1998 but have yet to win a World Series, despite some recent ambitious spending. Regardless, with its excellent spectator facilities, fine surroundings and agreeable climate, Petco Park is undoubtedly a very pleasant place to watch a ball game. Especially for dogs.

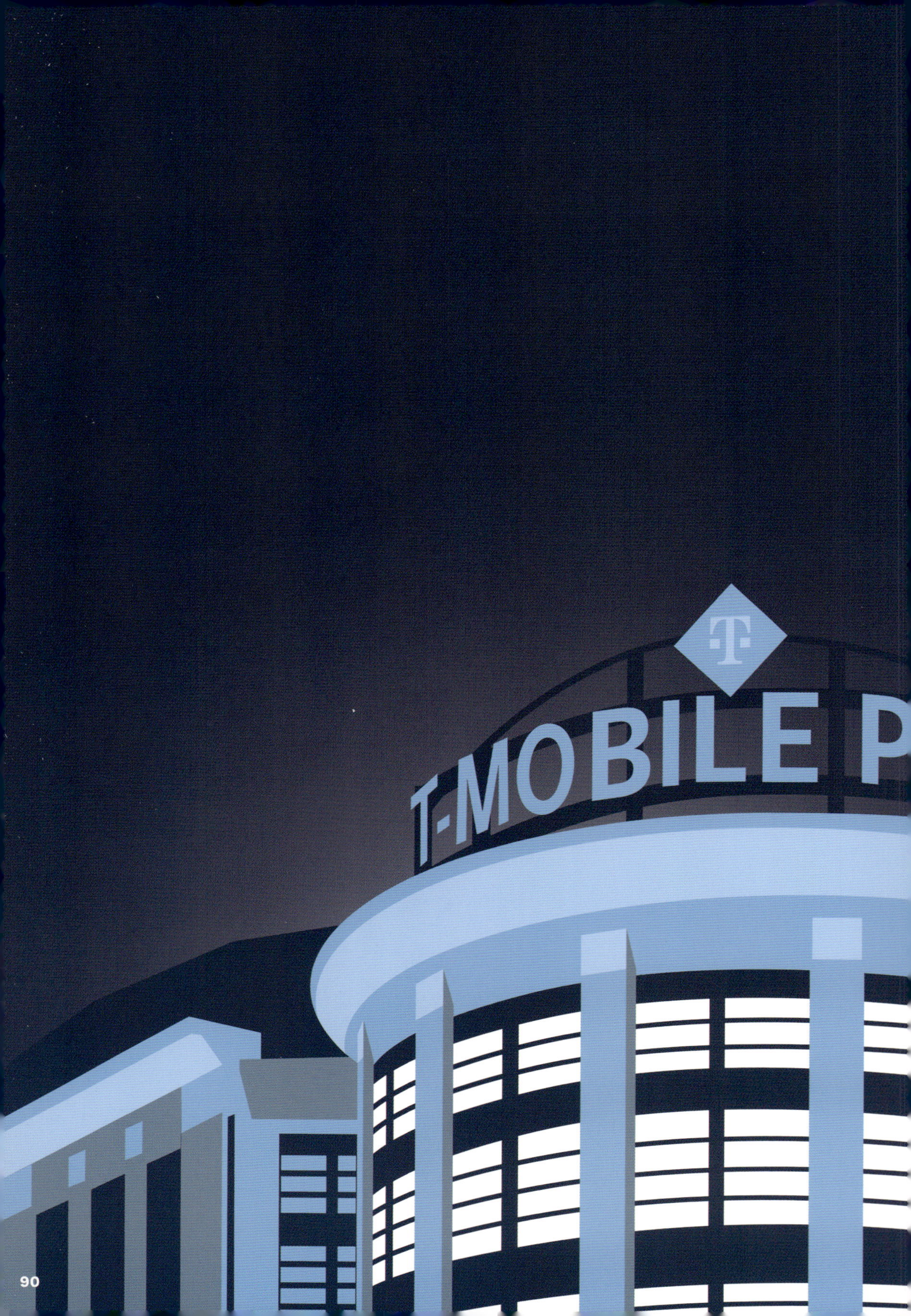
T-MOBILE P

'At the Corner of Edgar and Dave'

T-Mobile Park

Seattle, WA

The last new ballpark of the 20th century is a great place to watch baseball but it's not one of the more aesthetically pleasing ones. A roof was always going to be necessary, given Seattle's grungey weather, and this park has a rather clever retractable one. Rather than forming a sealed enclosure, it acts as an 'umbrella' and so retains the 'outdoor' feel even when it's closed. It is pretty substantial though, adding to the fairly industrial look of the building, which features a lot of exposed metal and some token brickwork.

The new park opened in 1999, next-door to their previous home; the even less pretty Kingdome, which was shared with the NFL's Seahawks. After the Kingdome was demolished, the Seahawks' impressive new stadium, now known as Lumen Field, emerged on the site and when viewed from Smith Tower or the Bainbridge Ferry, it literally and metaphorically puts the baseball stadium in the shade; rather like a younger, more glamorous sibling taking the spotlight in your family photos.

The Mariners entered MLB in 1977 and quickly established a reputation for losing; failing to achieve a winning record throughout their first 14 seasons and only reaching the playoffs for the first time in 1995. They did manage to get relatively close to playing in a World Series at their new home, losing to the Yankees in the ALCS in both 2000 and 2001, but it would be a staggering 21 years before Seattle returned to the playoffs after that.

Two bona fide Mariners legends transitioned from the Kingdome to the inaugural season at Safeco: Hall of Famers Ken Griffey Jr. and Edgar Martínez. Griffey departed after one season but returned ten years later for another two year stint. They are the only two Mariners to have their numbers officially 'retired' by the club. The Kingdome's 'Take Me

Out to the Bald Game' tradition, inspired by shaven-headed player, Jay Buhner, was also continued at Safeco, and over seven years, more than 22,000 fans gained free admission in return for having their own heads shaved at the park.

Safeco's third year saw the arrival of Japanese superstar, Ichiro Suzuki, who took the American League by storm in 2001, leading the team to the playoffs, topping the charts for steals and batting average, winning Rookie of the Year and MVP, and starting a ten-year consecutive run of All-Star nominations, Gold Glove Awards and 200-hit seasons.

The 'Ichiro Effect' sustained Seattle for over a decade and is perhaps best encapsulated by the 2010 occasion when he reached into the stands chasing a fly-ball and lightly collided with perhaps the most excitable young lady in the Pacific North-West region. Her exuberant and joyful reaction earned her the nickname 'Ichiro Girl' and videos of the incident have been viewed more than six million times. Twelve years later, she went heartwarmingly viral again after throwing an equally excited ceremonial first-pitch to Ichiro, on his induction into the Mariners Hall of Fame.

Despite their lack of team success, the Mariners have still been able to field some individual superstars, such as long-tenured Venezuelan pitcher, 'King' Félix Hernández. For his starts, sections of the park were designated as 'The King's Court', with ticket-holders receiving a special yellow t-shirt and a 'K' card to raise for each strikeout. In 2012, Hernández pitched the 23rd perfect game in MLB history, including 12 strikeouts, in a home victory over Tampa Bay.

Dave Niehaus, the Mariners' play-by-play announcer from the team's inception, sadly died in November 2010. On Opening Day 2011, local rapper, Macklemore, performed his own emotional tribute song 'My Oh My', named after Dave's oft-repeated exclamation in commentary; a phrase which also appears on an impressive statue inside the park depicting him at his announcer's desk. A nearby street was also designated 'Dave Niehaus Way South' in his honor and, as it intersects with the existing Edgar Martínez Drive South, the stadium is sometimes referred to as 'The Park at the Corner of Edgar and Dave'. T-Mobile took over official naming-rights in January 2019.

During the seventh-inning stretch, the Mariners have traditionally played 'Take Me Out to the Ball Game', before segueing into 'Louie Louie' by The Kingsmen. In 2022, the team began inserting Macklemore's 'Can't Hold Us' into the second slot instead, apparently after monitoring a positive reaction to it in previous broadcasts. Whilst some traditionalists consider this another example of data analytics ruining baseball, the Mariners coincidentally broke their long play-off drought at the end of that season. They remain the only current team never to have played in a World Series.

'Busch III'

Busch Stadium

St. Louis, MO

The Cardinals have won 11 World Series, second only to the Yankees, and have a reputation for doing things with class and style. That applies to their downtown ballpark too, which delivers all you would want in St. Louis: a view of the Gateway Arch, a decent field with good spectator facilities and someone saying "this Bud's for you".

The current stadium, the third to carry the Busch Stadium name, is a baseball-only facility, which shares part of the footprint of Busch Memorial Stadium ('Busch II'). League rules in 1953 prevented the owners from naming the original park 'Budweiser' but, although Anheuser-Busch sold the team in 1996, you can still see the Budweiser brand name atop the scoreboard and in the stadium's bars. The majestic Budweiser Clydesdale horses are also an integral part of opening day every year. They trot around the stadium, to the sound of 'Here Comes the King' from the famous Budweiser commercial, traditionally followed by a procession of Cardinals legends and the players. You'll also hear that jingle at the end of the seventh-inning of every game to signify that beer sales are about to end.

The new stadium opened on 10 April 2006, in what turned out to be a memorable season. Construction work was only fully completed in May, and in July a game was delayed by over two hours after a storm wreaked havoc on the stadium, injuring 30 people. The year ended well though, with the Cardinals winning their tenth World Series at the conclusion of a Fall Classic trilogy series against Detroit: the teams had previously faced off in 1934 and 1968, with the Cards winning the first and the Tigers the second. That was the first time for nearly 100 years that a team had won a World Series in their first year at a new park, although the Yankees repeated the feat in 2009.

The park itself is tastefully designed and its red brick façade fits in well with other local architecture, as well as the Cardinals' own Redbird imagery. Gate 3 on the west side of the stadium features an impressive gateway resembling the iconic Eads Bridge, which crosses the Mississippi River nearby, and a bronze statue to Stan 'The Man' Musial. Stan played for the Cardinals from 1941 to 1963, winning three World Series, and was an All-Star 24 times from 1943 onwards, despite there being no game in 1945 and there being two games in seasons 1959-1962.

The Ballpark Village development in the streets beyond left-field significantly improved the surrounding area and helps to enhance the gameday experience for fans. It first opened in 2014 and includes a Hall of Fame and Museum, as well as the Cardinals Nation Rooftop and Budweiser Terrace, which are incorporated into the stadium. Although some high-rise buildings have sprung up around the perimeter, the stadium's views of the green-domed Old Courthouse and the Gateway Arch have been preserved.

During September 2022, the Cardinals gave away one of the most sought-after baseball collectible sets ever: interlocking bobbleheads of long-time team-mates Adam Wainwright, Yadier Molina and Albert Pujols. Yadier, the most successful of the Molina catching dynasty, and Pujols, ranked second in major league history in runs batted in and total bases, behind only Hank Aaron, had intimated in advance that they would be retiring at the end of the season. Both men had collected World Series rings as Cardinals in 2006 and 2011, but pitcher Wainwright missed out on the second triumph due to Tommy John surgery.

That win in 2011 only came about after the Cardinals had hauled back Atlanta's 10.5 game lead late in the season and clinched the Wild Card on a memorable 'Game 162' night. The following NL Divisional Series gave birth to the legend of the 'Rally Squirrel' after the same rodent interrupted games at Busch on consecutive days, helping the Cardinals overcome the Phillies 3-2, before going on to beat Milwaukee and Texas. The squirrel was eventually captured and released into the wild and was depicted on its own Topps baseball card in 2018.

In the final game of the 2022 regular season, pre-game tributes were paid to Molina and Pujols and, when Wainwright was pulled from the game in the fifth-inning, both were also taken out, to a standing ovation. Their careers ended a few days later when the Phillies beat the squirrel-free Cardinals in the Wild Card Series, but Wainwright has declared his intention to continue his career beyond 2022.

'The Trop'

Tropicana Field

St. Petersburg, FL

The lease for this largely unloved stadium in St. Petersburg is due to expire in 2027, and although the owners and local authorities on both sides of Tampa Bay appear committed to finding a replacement, funding and location may yet prove a bridge too far.

The Florida Suncoast Dome opened in 1990 but by the time the Tampa Bay Devil Rays arrived in 1998, the ballpark design revolution was underway, leaving the newly-renamed Tropicana Field already looking something of an ugly duckling.

A roof is essential for summer baseball in humid Florida but tracking the ball against the slanted fixed roof can be challenging and the rings supporting the dome even have their own ground rules specifying what happens when a fly-ball hits one.

Since exorcising the 'devil' from the team's name in 2008, the Rays have achieved remarkable on-field success on a limited budget, including two World Series appearances. The venue's most memorable moment came on the last day of the 2011 regular season. After a dramatic comeback and a simultaneous Red Sox 'choke' in Baltimore, the Rays sensationally walked-off into the playoffs when Evan Longoria's home run cleared the low fence in left-field into a party area now known as '162 Landing'.

Despite these heroics and fan-friendly features like the 'touch tank' in the outfield containing actual Cownose Rays, the club have been unable to draw sufficient numbers to the west side of Tampa Bay, with bridge traffic bottlenecks an issue. After a split-season two-city plan with Montreal was rejected, it seems likely the franchise will rebuild on-site but a move to Tampa or out-of-state is still possible.

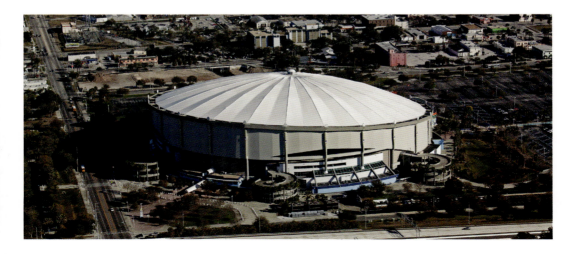

'Made for the Shade'

Globe Life Field

Arlington, TX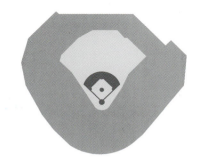

They only moved about 0.3 miles and changed the last word from 'Park' to 'Field', but there's a world of difference between the Texas Rangers' old and new parks.

The 1994 'Park' version still has the look of a classic ballpark, with its intricate red brick façade, lakeside location and period features. It's now known as Choctaw Stadium and has been reconfigured for rectangular sports like XFL, soccer and rugby. That park's Achilles' heel was the lack of protection from the summer sun, which made the left-field seats a no-go area most of the time and day games largely insufferable.

The $1.2bn replacement, opened in 2020, has a giant single-panel retractable roof and air-con, which delivers a much more pleasant spectator experience. Aerial views of the park are not favorable in comparison to the old park or the opulent Cowboys stadium next door, but the designers have made every effort to give it walk-up curb appeal, through translucent clerestories and extensive use of Ethylene tetrafluoroethylene, a fluorine-based plastic. It actually looks quite impressive, particularly at night, although it bears little resemblance to an old-school park.

Once inside, the new venue is a great place to watch a game, and fan feedback seems to be uniformly positive. It has plenty of modern amenities and tricks, including a pitcher's mound which can be lowered hydraulically for non-baseball events. The upper outfield concourse is a gem, with a delightful arched skybridge and seats that appear to float in front of windows.

The new park hosted the World Series in its first year, but sadly for Rangers fans, it was a neutral Covid-bubble event featuring the Dodgers and Rays.

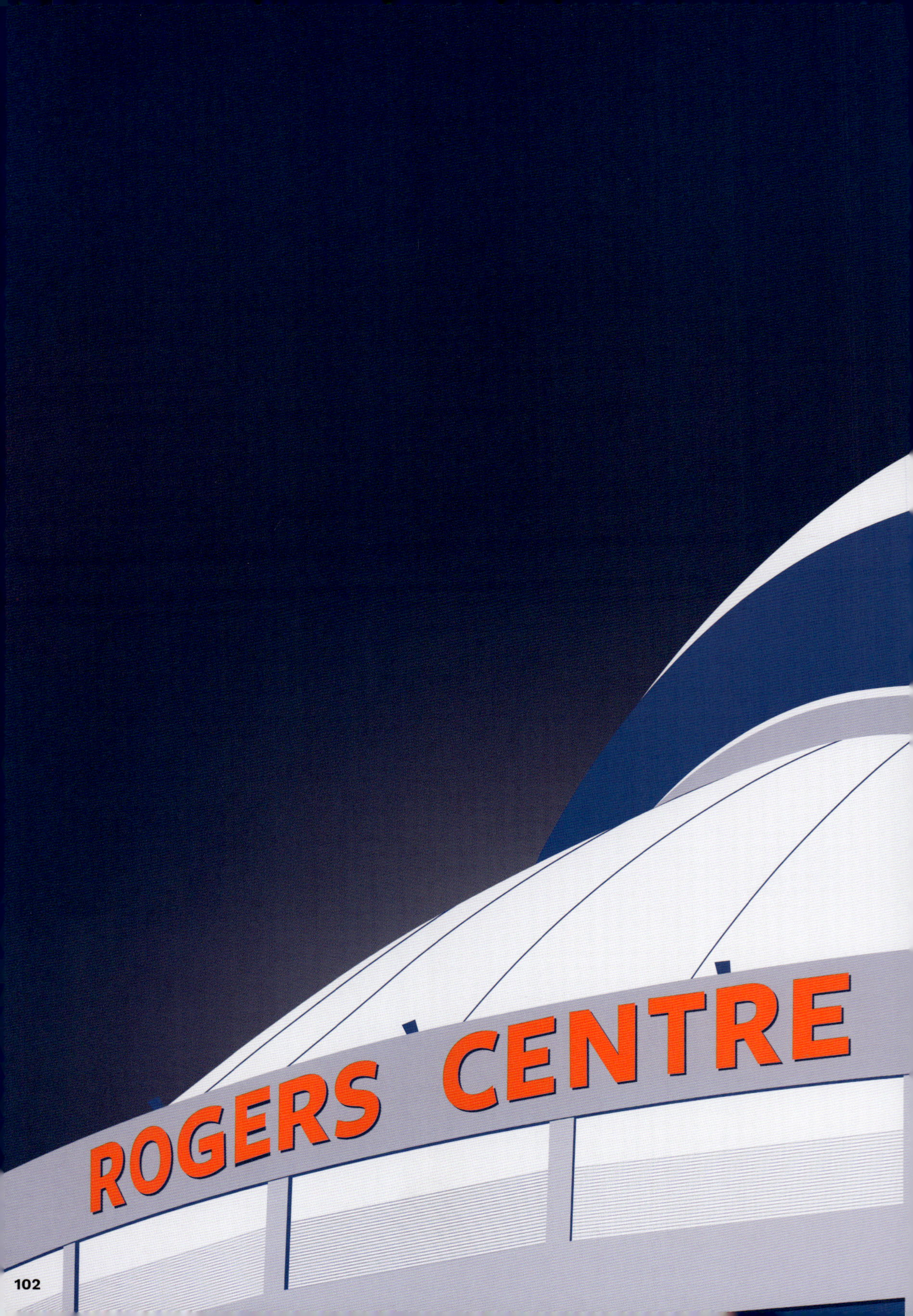
ROGERS CENTRE

'OK Blue Jays'

Rogers Centre

Toronto, ON 🇨🇦

They say absence makes the heart grow fonder and maybe folks appreciated the Rogers Centre a little bit more after Covid-related border restrictions prevented the Toronto Blue Jays from playing there during most of the 2020 and 2021 seasons. Whilst the downtown location is almost perfect, the expanse of concrete, the almost-circular multi-sports layout and the artificial turf have resulted in at least a passing resemblance to the now-extinct 'cookie-cutter' stadiums - and there has been some in Toronto casting envious eyes at the prettier, more-modern ballparks popping up across America.

During their exile, the Jays played most of their 'home' games in Buffalo and filled the seats with cardboard cut-outs of actual fans during closed-doors games. Geddy Lee of prog-rock gods, Rush, featured prominently, but the best spot was reserved for the legendary but anonymous elderly woman known only as 'Home Plate Lady'. She has been a very familiar figure at Rogers Centre for many years with a seat directly in line of shot for the TV cameras on almost every pitch. She famously never flinches when a foul-tip ball strikes the barrier in front of her and, in Buffalo, the Jays even dressed her cut-out in one of her signature scarves each day. On the Blue Jays' return to Rogers Centre in July 2021, the sight of 'Nonna' taking her seat after throwing a ceremonial first pitch drew an emotional ovation and somehow symbolized that everything was going to be OK again in Toronto.

When it opened, mid-way through the 1989 season, the SkyDome was the first major team-sports stadium in North America with a functional, fully retractable roof. It is comparatively rare for the roof to be closed during baseball's summer months and that facilitates a stunning view of the giant CN Tower looming over the outfield. You can see into the stadium from the

Tower's observation decks and the brave can even take a look from the frightening EdgeWalk open-air platform.

'Kiss Cam' is a regular feature at most sporting events, but it is generally expected that participants will stick to kissing and not go beyond 'first base' in the 'Meat Loaf' scale of baseball sex-euphemisms. A hotel built into the stadium's outfield structure features some suites with full-length windows over-looking the playing field and on one occasion shortly after opening, the stadium lights inadvertently illuminated a couple going for an 'inside-the-park home run' in a darkened room. Guests are now required to take appropriate precautions and sign a disclaimer.

The Blue Jays had immediate success in their new home, reaching the American League pennant game in 1989 and 1991, and becoming the first MLB club to draw over four million fans in a season. In 1992, they were even better and became the first Canadian team to win the World Series. The SkyDome's greatest moment came the following year when Joe Carter's walk-off home run in Game 6 of the 1993 World Series made the Jays back-to-back world champions. They have not reached the Fall Classic since and it would be a long 22 years before the Blue Jays even made the playoffs again; an achievement most remembered for José Bautista's outrageous bat-flip after a go-ahead home run in Toronto against Texas in the 2015 ALDS.

Despite some great slugging seasons in Toronto, Bautista was never able to join the exclusive club of players who have hit a home run into the towering fifth deck of the stadium. Jose Canseco was the first to do it in 1989 and nearly 30 years later, Austin Meadows and Brandon Lowe of the Tampa Bay Rays became only the 21st and 22nd hitters to achieve the feat, with both of their shots coming in the same inning.

The Blue Jays traditionally host a home game on Canada Day, when they wear red jerseys instead of their usual blue. Toronto is the only club to feature two national anthems before every game, with 'O Canada' also sung in French on occasions. The Jays also double-up on their seventh-inning stretch songs with the quirky 'OK Blue Jays' coming before the traditional TMOTTBG.

After the Toronto Argonauts football team moved out in 2015, the stadium's moveable seating decks and field surface were re-configured exclusively for baseball, and in 2022, the Jays announced a $300m renovation project which would appear to secure the building's future. Improvements planned include raised bullpens, seats closer to the action and 'social' areas, with the stated intention to finally "transform the stadium into a ballpark".

'All the Presidents' Men'

Nationals Park

Washington, DC

When Nationals Park hosted its inaugural regular season game on 30 March 2008, local resident George W. Bush of 1600 Pennsylvania Avenue, threw out the ceremonial opening pitch. Two years later, White Sox fan, Barack Obama, did the same, continuing a loosely-observed tradition of US presidents pitching on opening day, which was started by William H. Taft 100 years previously.

Of course, there's not always been a team in Washington for the president to visit. The original Senators / Nationals left for Minnesota in 1960 and the 1961 expansion Senators which replaced them moved to Texas in 1972. MLB relocated the Montreal Expos to Washington to become the 'new' Nationals in 2005, initially based at RFK Stadium.

The new park was built using steel, glass and concrete and is tastefully designed to integrate into its surroundings beside the rapidly revitalizing Navy Yard area and the Anacostia riverfront. As the stadium's lights are attached to the upper canopy, there are no distinctive light towers to guide you to the park. In fact, like the city's NHL / NBA arena, it's so unobtrusive, it scarcely looks like a stadium at all, unless you are approaching the distinctively-glassed home plate entrance, which few supporters do.

Once inside, the park presents a very pleasant spectator experience. The limited views of the city's landmarks are gradually being obscured by local developments, but fans have good field sightlines from the stands and the trendy Loft and Brewhouse 'hang-out' areas.

One of the dilemmas of modern stadium building is how many 'signature' features to build in. Too few can lead to a feeling of blandness, but overdoing it can be perceived as contrived and gimmicky. Nationals Park leans towards the former but some clusters of Japanese Cherry Blossom Trees

provide regional flavor and short-lived early-season Hanami. First Lady Helen Taft and the Japanese Ambassador's wife planted the first of the District's distinctive Cherry Blossom Trees just a few days before Fenway Park opened in 1912.

Reflecting the Navy Yard location, the club host visiting military personnel in premium seats and acknowledge them in a 'Salute to Service' at the end of the third-inning, while home runs and wins are celebrated using the sound of a submarine dive horn.

In one of modern baseball's finest new traditions, giant foam caricatures of the four presidents portrayed on Mount Rushmore (Thomas Jefferson, George Washington, Abraham Lincoln and Teddy Roosevelt) take part in a Presidents Race during the fourth-inning of every home game. As a result of dirty tactics and various WWE-style shenanigans, Teddy Roosevelt did not legally win a single race in his first 525 attempts over seven years. A wide-spread and vociferous 'Let Teddy Win' insurgency gained notable support from the Nationals' Jayson Werth, who twice staged mid-race interventions, before Teddy eventually triumphed in the last game of the 2012 regular season.

A JFK figure made a one-off appearance in 2011 and Presidents Taft, Coolidge and Hoover have also taken part, before being 'retired' to Palm Beach for Spring Training. The Nationals traditionally host an 11am home game on Independence Day when the race becomes a flag-carrying procession, and should any ball game reach the thirteenth-inning, the presidents return for a second race.

The new Nationals did not have their first winning season until 2012, but their win streak continued for the next eight years, culminating in a World Series triumph in 2019. Due to Covid restrictions, fans were not able to properly celebrate the team receiving their rings and raising the banner, although most of the team were able to attend the traditional White House visit in November 2019. Over the next two seasons, the championship-winning roster was substantially dismantled and the team has reverted to a Teddy-like losing record.

In 2010, the Nationals unveiled a 'Ring of Honor' to celebrate significant former players. Inductees included stars from the current franchise's origins in Montreal, plus representatives from previous Washington clubs, including several from the celebrated Homestead Grays of the Negro Leagues.

In 2018, Jayson Werth became the first of the post-2005 Nationals to be inducted. It is likely he will be joined by members of the World Series-winning team in due course, most prominently 'Mr National', Ryan Zimmerman. He was the team's first draft-pick after relocation and hit a walk-off home run to win that first ever game at Nationals Park. Before retiring in 2021, he spent his entire career with the Nationals, including the 2019 World Championship. The team retired his #11 in 2022.

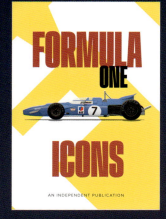

www.aspenbooks.co.uk

THE BASEBALL STADIUM GUIDE

Written by Iain McArthur
Designed by Daniel Brawn

ASPEN BOOKS

© 2023. Published by Aspen Books, an imprint of Pillar Box Red Publishing Ltd. Printed in India.

This is an independent publication. It has no connection with any of the baseball teams featured or with any organisation or individual connected in any way whatsoever with the baseball teams or with Major League Baseball.

Any quotes within this publication which are attributed to anyone connected to a baseball team or Major League Baseball have been sourced from other publications or from the internet and, as such, are a matter of public record.

Whilst every effort has been made to ensure the accuracy of information within this publication, the publisher shall have no liability to any person or entity with respect to any inaccuracy, misleading information, loss or damage caused directly or indirectly by the information contained within this book.
The views expressed are solely those of the author and do not reflect the opinions of Aspen Books. All rights reserved.

ISBN: 978-1-914536-71-7
Images © Alamy